A GUIDED ALTER[N...]
TO GUILT-DRIVEN JO[...]

the GUILT-FREE Journal

JAN SILVIOUS

ILLUSTRATED BY PHILLIP RODGERS

AMG Publishers

ISBN: 0-89957-321-5

Scripture Quotations come from the following translations:

Text and Cover Design by Phillip Rodgers

Printed in Canada
06 05 04 03 02 01 –T– 6 5 4 3 2 1

INTRODUCTION

Welcome to journaling! For all who have started journals only to leave them on the shelf after two days—this journal is for you. There is no right way to compose your journal, nor is there a wrong way. This is your journal to enjoy and love. This is your journal to record your thoughts, your prayers, and your memories. The only rule-maker is you . . . therefore, no guilt!

☑ Skipping a few days is not a failure. You are just giving your mind space.

☑ No matter how much or how little you record, save it. It is part of your history.

☑ Sometimes you may feel a need to write something extremely private about yourself or someone you know and love. Create a code system to disguise names or subjects that are of a sensitive nature. A code system prevents embarrassment and hurt feelings if, perchance, someone happens to pick up your journal.

☑ Keep your journal in a handy location.

☑ Enjoy! If it becomes drudgery, you've missed the point.

BLESSINGS,
JAN

"Two things I ask of you, O Lord; do not refuse me before I die: Keep falsehood and lies far from me; give me neither poverty nor riches, but give me only my daily bread. Otherwise, I may have too much and disown you and say, 'Who is the Lord?' Or I may become poor and steal, and so dishonor the name of my God."

PROVERBS 30:7–9 (NIV)

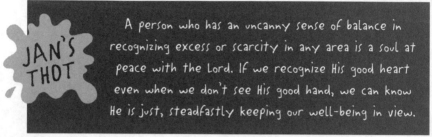

JAN'S THOT

A person who has an uncanny sense of balance in recognizing excess or scarcity in any area is a soul at peace with the Lord. If we recognize His good heart even when we don't see His good hand, we can know He is just, steadfastly keeping our well-being in view.

My personal thoughts are...

_____

_____

_____

_____

_____

_____

_____

_____

_____

_____

_____

_____

Father God, I come to You with my
prayer today.

_____
_____
_____
_____
_____
_____
_____
_____

I thank You especially for_____

_____
_____
_____
_____

I love you for_____

_____
_____
_____
_____
_____
_____
_____
_____

I lift these people
before you...

1 _____
2 _____
3 _____
4 _____
5 _____
6 _____
7 _____
8 _____
9 _____
10 _____
11 _____
12 _____
13 _____
14 _____
15 _____

"Who is the man (or woman) who desires life, and loves many days, that he may see good? Depart from evil, and do good; seek peace and pursue it."

PSALM 34:12–14 (NKJV)

JAN'S THOT

If you seek peace and pursue it, you will find it. Peace doesn't just fall out of the sky. It is your choice to go after it!

My personal thoughts are...

_____
_____
_____
_____
_____
_____
_____
_____
_____
_____
_____
_____
_____
_____

Father, I want to live life to the fullest. Show me how I might be blocking my own way.

Give me a willing heart to...

_____
_____
_____
_____
_____

I look to you to provide...

_____
_____
_____
_____
_____

I pray for these people...

_____
_____
_____
_____

I love you for...

_____
_____
_____
_____
_____

I thank you for what you have done for me...

_____
_____
_____
_____
_____
_____

I need you to...

_____
_____
_____
_____
_____

"Many are the plans in a man's heart, but it is the Lord's purpose that prevails."
PROVERBS 19:21 (NIV)

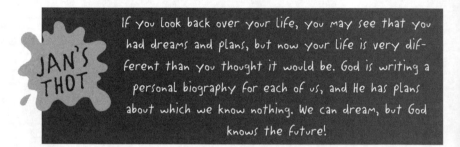

JAN'S THOT

If you look back over your life, you may see that you had dreams and plans, but now your life is very different than you thought it would be. God is writing a personal biography for each of us, and He has plans about which we know nothing. We can dream, but God knows the future!

My personal thoughts are...

_____

_____

_____

_____

_____

_____

_____

_____

_____

_____

_____

_____

_____

Lord God, I thank You for _____

~~~~~~~~~~~~~~~~~~~~~~~~~~~~~~~~~~~~~~~

~~~~~~~~~~~~~~~~~~~~~~~~~~~~~~~~~~~~~~~

~~~~~~~~~~~~~~~~~~~~~~~~~~~~~~~~~~~~~~~

~~~~~~~~~~~~~~~~~~~~~~~~~~~~~~~~~~~~~~~

~~~~~~~~~~~~~~~~~~~~~~~~~~~~~~~~~~~~~~~

I pray for_____

~~~~~~~~~~~~~~~~~~~~~~~~~~~~~~~~~~~~~~~

~~~~~~~~~~~~~~~~~~~~~~~~~~~~~~~~~~~~~~~

~~~~~~~~~~~~~~~~~~~~~~~~~~~~~~~~~~~~~~~

~~~~~~~~~~~~~~~~~~~~~~~~~~~~~~~~~~~~~~~

~~~~~~~~~~~~~~~~~~~~~~~~~~~~~~~~~~~~~~~

I love You for_____

~~~~~~~~~~~~~~~~~~~~~~~~~~~~~~~~~~~~~~~

~~~~~~~~~~~~~~~~~~~~~~~~~~~~~~~~~~~~~~~

~~~~~~~~~~~~~~~~~~~~~~~~~~~~~~~~~~~~~~~

~~~~~~~~~~~~~~~~~~~~~~~~~~~~~~~~~~~~~~~

~~~~~~~~~~~~~~~~~~~~~~~~~~~~~~~~~~~~~~~

~~~~~~~~~~~~~~~~~~~~~~~~~~~~~~~~~~~~~~~

~~~~~~~~~~~~~~~~~~~~~~~~~~~~~~~~~~~~~~~

~~~~~~~~~~~~~~~~~~~~~~~~~~~~~~~~~~~~~~~

~~~~~~~~~~~~~~~~~~~~~~~~~~~~~~~~~~~~~~~

I lift these people before you...

1 _____
2 _____
3 _____
4 _____
5 _____
6 _____
7 _____
8 _____
9 _____
10 _____
11 _____
12 _____
13 _____
14 _____
15 _____

Today's Date _____

"Being confident of this very thing, that He who has begun a good work in you will complete it until the day of Jesus Christ."

PHILIPPIANS 1:6 (NKJV)

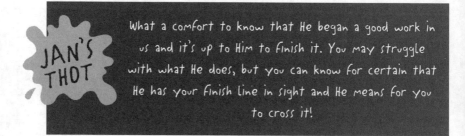

JAN'S THOT

What a comfort to know that He began a good work in us and it's up to Him to finish it. You may struggle with what He does, but you can know for certain that He has your finish line in sight and He means for you to cross it!

My personal thoughts are...

_____

_____

_____

_____

_____

_____

_____

_____

_____

_____

_____

Father God, I want to become more confident in You.

These are the things that scare me:

_____
_____
_____
_____
_____
_____

These are the places where I become weak:

_____
_____
_____
_____

I believe that You can. . .

_____
_____
_____
_____
_____

Thank you for beginning a good work in me. Since I have become a Christian, I have grown in these areas:

_____
_____
_____
_____
_____
_____
_____
_____

I love you for. . .

_____
_____
_____
_____

*"The secret of the Lord is for those who fear Him,
And He will make them know His covenant."*

PSALM 25:14 (NASB)

JAN'S THOT

Have you ever thought on how you came to know the things of God? He has chosen to bring the knowledge of Himself only to those who have made a covenant with Him. Because spiritual things are spiritually understood, you know things non-believers don't know. That doesn't make you better. It just means you are related to the One who wants you to know His secrets.

What secrets of the Lord are dear to you?

_____

_____

_____

_____

_____

_____

_____

_____

_____

_____

_____

_____

Father, I reverence You. I believe You are...

_____

_____

_____

_____

_____

_____

_____

I have experienced Your...

_____

_____

_____

_____

_____

_____

I love You for_____

_____

_____

_____

_____

_____

_____

_____

My goals for the next few days:

_____

_____

_____

_____

_____

_____

_____

_____

_____

_____

_____

_____

_____

_____

Today's Date _____

"I would have lost heart, unless I had believed that I would see the goodness of the LORD in the land of the living. Wait on the LORD; be of good courage, and He shall strengthen your heart; wait, I say, on the LORD!"

PSALM 27:13, 14 (NKJV)

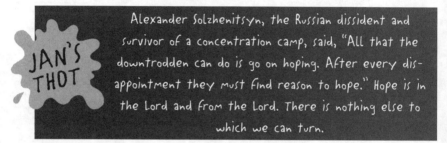

JAN'S THOT

Alexander Solzhenitsyn, the Russian dissident and survivor of a concentration camp, said, "All that the downtrodden can do is go on hoping. After every disappointment they must find reason to hope." Hope is in the Lord and from the Lord. There is nothing else to which we can turn.

My personal thoughts are...

_____

_____

_____

_____

_____

_____

_____

_____

_____

_____

_____

_____

_____

_____

Lord, I look to You for hope.

Here are my major concerns today:

_____
_____
_____
_____

_____

This is my greatest fear:

_____
_____
_____
_____
_____

I love You for_____
_____
_____
_____
_____

I lift these people before you...

1 _____
2 _____
3 _____
4 _____
5 _____
6 _____
7 _____
8 _____
9 _____
10 _____
11 _____
12 _____
13 _____
14 _____
15 _____

"But as it is written: 'Eye has not seen, nor ear heard, nor have entered into the heart of man the things which God has prepared for those who love Him.'"

1 CORINTHIANS 2:9 (NKJV)

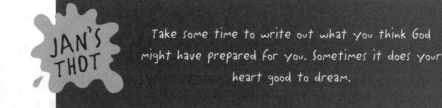

JAN'S THOT

Take some time to write out what you think God might have prepared for you. Sometimes it does your heart good to dream.

_____

_____

_____

_____

_____

_____

_____

_____

_____

_____

_____

_____

_____

Father, I want to know how to love You more.

~~~~~~
~~~~~~
~~~~~~
~~~~~~

I long to know what You have prepared for me.

~~~~~~
~~~~~~
~~~~~~
~~~~~~
~~~~~~

I pray for these people with love:

~~~~~~
~~~~~~
~~~~~~
~~~~~~
~~~~~~
~~~~~~
~~~~~~

I need to ask for forgiveness from:

1 ~~~~~~~~~~~~~~~~~~~~~~
2 ~~~~~~~~~~~~~~~~~~~~~~
3 ~~~~~~~~~~~~~~~~~~~~~~
4 ~~~~~~~~~~~~~~~~~~~~~~
5 ~~~~~~~~~~~~~~~~~~~~~~
6 ~~~~~~~~~~~~~~~~~~~~~~
7 ~~~~~~~~~~~~~~~~~~~~~~
8 ~~~~~~~~~~~~~~~~~~~~~~
9 ~~~~~~~~~~~~~~~~~~~~~~
10 ~~~~~~~~~~~~~~~~~~~~~
11 ~~~~~~~~~~~~~~~~~~~~~
12 ~~~~~~~~~~~~~~~~~~~~~
13 ~~~~~~~~~~~~~~~~~~~~~
14 ~~~~~~~~~~~~~~~~~~~~~
15 ~~~~~~~~~~~~~~~~~~~~~

"Those who sow in tears shall reap in joy. He who continually goes forth weeping, bearing seed for sowing, shall doubtless come again with rejoicing, bringing his sheaves with him."

PSALM 126:5, 6 (NKJV)

JAN'S THOT

Are you crying about something in your life? Are you looking for answers? Are you searching for help? God will not disappoint you. He may not do what you want Him to do, but you can know He always has your very best interest in His heart.

My personal thoughts are...

_____

_____

_____

_____

_____

_____

_____

_____

_____

_____

_____

_____

_____

Lord, I want to be a person who is trustworthy.

I invite You to work in my
life to strengthen me
about . . .

_____
_____
_____
_____
_____
_____
_____

I love You for . . .

_____
_____
_____
_____
_____
_____
_____
_____
_____

I invite You to work in a
situation that is troubling:

_____
_____
_____
_____
_____
_____
_____
_____
_____

I thank You that You love me
and I ask You to work a deeper
love for You into my heart.

_____
_____
_____
_____
_____
_____
_____

"There is therefore now no condemnation to those who are in Christ Jesus, who do not walk according to the flesh, but according to the Spirit."

ROMANS 8:1 (NKJV)

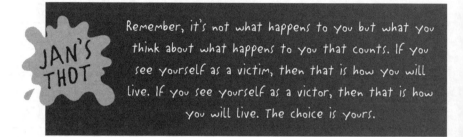

JAN'S THOT

Remember, it's not what happens to you but what you think about what happens to you that counts. If you see yourself as a victim, then that is how you will live. If you see yourself as a victor, then that is how you will live. The choice is yours.

How do you perceive yourself?

_____
_____
_____
_____
_____
_____
_____
_____
_____
_____
_____
_____

Father, I want to be free of any condemnation.

These are the ways I tend to "walk according to the flesh":

_____

_____

_____

_____

_____

_____

_____

I confess that I have 'thought' like a victim by thinking that I am not good enough for . . .

_____

_____

_____

_____

_____

_____

_____

I ask You to forgive me and to remind me that these behaviors and thoughts go against You. Amen.

I need to forgive these people:

1 _____

2 _____

3 _____

4 _____

5 _____

6 _____

7 _____

8 _____

9 _____

10 _____

11 _____

12 _____

13 _____

14 _____

15 _____

Surprise!!!!!

Go outside and notice the ways that God is speaking to you through nature today!

Notice the sounds as well as the sights.

What do you hear?

_____

_____

_____

_____

_____

What do you see?

_____

_____

_____

_____

_____

Read the following passage and thank God for speaking to you through His creation!

"The heavens are telling the glory of God; they are a marvelous display of his crafts-manship. Day and night they keep on telling about God. Without a sound or word, silent in the skies, their message reaches out to all the world. The sun lives in the heavens where God placed it and moves out across the skies as radiant as a bride-groom going to his wedding, or as joyous as an athlete looking forward to a race! The sun crosses the heavens from end to end, and nothing can hide from its heat."

PSALMS 19:1–6 (LB)

_____

_____

_____

_____

_____

_____

_____

_____

_____

_____

_____

_____

"Therefore, if anyone is in Christ, he is a new creation: old things have passed away, behold, all things have become new."

2 CORINTHIANS 5:17 (NKJV)

JAN'S THOT

Do you have any relationships in your life that keep you from fully trusting and worshiping God? If so, you are probably caught up in an unhealthy dependency. Either you are dependent on another person(s) or he/she is dependent on you. God has created us to be interdependent with one another and totally dependent on Him. That is how it works best in relationships with God—and with each other.

Describe your relationships with God and others.

_____

_____

_____

_____

_____

_____

_____

_____

_____

_____

_____

_____

Lord, I want to praise You today for...

_____

_____

_____

_____

_____

_____

_____

_____

I love You for_____

_____

_____

_____

_____

_____

_____

_____

I ask you to intervene in my relation-
ship(s) with:_____

_____

_____

_____

_____

_____

I pray for my rela-
tionships with the
following people:

1 _____

2 _____

3 _____

4 _____

5 _____

6 _____

7 _____

8 _____

9 _____

10 _____

11 _____

12 _____

13 _____

14 _____

15 _____

"Trust in the LORD
with all your
heart, And lean
not on your own
understanding."

Proverbs 3:5 (NKJV)

Today's Date _____

"For I know that my Redeemer lives, and He shall stand at last on the earth."
JOB 19:25 (NKJV)

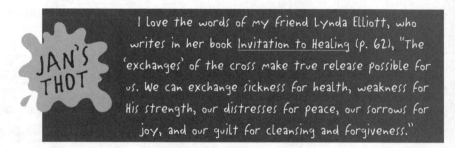

JAN'S THOT

I love the words of my friend Lynda Elliott, who writes in her book <u>Invitation to Healing</u> (p. 62), "The 'exchanges' of the cross make true release possible for us. We can exchange sickness for health, weakness for His strength, our distresses for peace, our sorrows for joy, and our guilt for cleansing and forgiveness."

My personal thoughts are...

_____

_____

_____

_____

_____

_____

_____

_____

_____

_____

_____

_____

_____

Father God, I praise You for sending Jesus to be my Redeemer.

I know that in Him I have been given...

_____
_____
_____
_____
_____

I confess the following sins to You:

_____
_____
_____
_____
_____

I love You for_____
_____
_____
_____
_____
_____
_____
_____

My heart is heavy for the following people who desperately need to know the Savior:

1 _____
2 _____
3 _____
4 _____
5 _____
6 _____
7 _____
8 _____
9 _____
10 _____
11 _____
12 _____
13 _____
14 _____
15 _____
16 _____
17 _____
18 _____
19 _____
20 _____

"Blessed be the God and Father of our Lord Jesus Christ, the Father of mercies and God of all comfort, who comforts us in all our tribulation, that we may be able to comfort those who are in any trouble, with the comfort with which we ourselves are comforted by God."

2 CORINTHIANS 13:4 (NKJV)

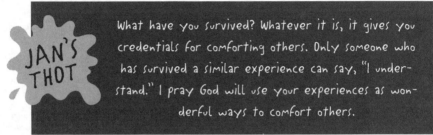

JAN'S THOT

What have you survived? Whatever it is, it gives you credentials for comforting others. Only someone who has survived a similar experience can say, "I understand." I pray God will use your experiences as wonderful ways to comfort others.

My personal thoughts are...

_____

_____

_____

_____

_____

_____

_____

_____

_____

_____

_____

father, I thank You for the
way You got me through . . .

_____
_____
_____
_____
_____
_____
_____
_____
_____
_____

I learned to trust You for...

_____
_____
_____
_____
_____
_____
_____
_____
_____
_____

I pray for_____
_____
_____
_____
_____
_____
_____
_____
_____
_____
_____
_____
_____
_____
_____

I love You for_____
_____
_____
_____
_____
_____
_____
_____
_____
_____

"The name of the LORD is a strong tower; the righteous run to it and are safe."
PROVERBS 18:10 (NIV)

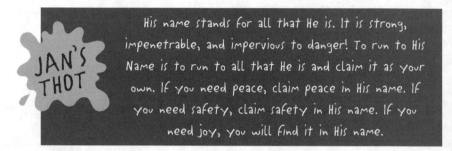

JAN'S THOT

His name stands for all that He is. It is strong, impenetrable, and impervious to danger! To run to His Name is to run to all that He is and claim it as your own. If you need peace, claim peace in His name. If you need safety, claim safety in His name. If you need joy, you will find it in His name.

My personal thoughts are...

_____
_____
_____
_____
_____
_____
_____
_____
_____
_____
_____
_____
_____

Father God, thank You that You are...

_____

_____

_____

_____

to me.

I ask You to speak to me about...

_____

_____

_____

_____

_____

_____

_____

I love You for_____

_____

_____

_____

_____

_____

_____

_____

_____

My objectives for
the next week are:

1 _____

2 _____

3 _____

4 _____

5 _____

6 _____

7 _____

8 _____

9 _____

10 _____

11 _____

12 _____

13 _____

14 _____

15 _____

"For whatever is born of God overcomes the world. And this is the victory that has overcome the world—our faith. Who is he who overcomes the world, but he who believes that Jesus is the Son of God?"

1 JOHN 5:4, 5 (KJV)

JAN'S THOT

Early in my Christian experience I learned that faith is taking God at His Word. This definition has affected my entire walk with Him. What is your definition of faith? How does it affect your relationship with the Lord?

My personal thoughts on faith are...

_____
_____
_____
_____
_____
_____
_____
_____
_____
_____
_____
_____

Heavenly Father, my faith is weak when...

_____
_____
_____
_____
_____
_____
_____
_____

I bring the names of these I love before You:

_____
_____
_____
_____

I thank You for _____
_____
_____
_____
_____

I bring the names of these I know need Your touch:

1 _____
2 _____
3 _____
4 _____
5 _____
6 _____
7 _____
8 _____
9 _____
10 _____
11 _____
12 _____
13 _____
14 _____
15 _____

"I will instruct you and teach you in the way you should go; I will guide you with my eye."
PSALM 32:8 (NKJV)

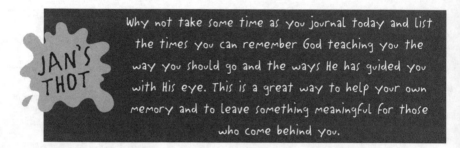

JAN'S THOT

Why not take some time as you journal today and list the times you can remember God teaching you the way you should go and the ways He has guided you with His eye. This is a great way to help your own memory and to leave something meaningful for those who come behind you.

My thoughts on God teaching me and leading me are...

_____

_____

_____

_____

_____

_____

_____

_____

_____

_____

_____

_____

Father, thank You that You always have...

_____
_____
_____
_____
_____
_____
_____

I love You for_____
_____
_____
_____
_____
_____
_____

I pray for_____
_____

_____
_____
_____
_____
_____
_____

I lift these people before you...

1 _____
2 _____
3 _____
4 _____
5 _____
6 _____
7 _____
8 _____
9 _____
10 _____
11 _____
12 _____
13 _____
14 _____
15 _____

"Those who are wise shall shine like the brightness of the firmament, and those who turn many to righteousness like the stars for ever and ever."

DANIEL 12:3 (NKJV)

JAN'S THOT

Knowing God and knowing His ways through His Word are the only ways to live safely in a world full of extremes. If you don't have peace about something, you have probably gone to an extreme. Think about it.

My personal thoughts are...

_____

_____

_____

_____

_____

_____

_____

_____

_____

_____

_____

_____

_____

Father, I thank You for the
wisdom You have given me
about _____

_____

_____

_____

_____

_____

_____

_____

_____

_____

_____

I thank You for_____

_____

_____

_____

_____

_____

_____

_____

_____

_____

_____

_____

_____

_____

_____

I pray for_____

_____

_____

_____

_____

_____

_____

_____

_____

_____

_____

I love You for_____

_____

_____

_____

_____

_____

_____

_____

_____

_____

_____

_____

_____

Today's Date _____

"Evening and morning and at noon I will pray, and cry aloud, and He shall hear my voice."
PSALM 55:17 (NKJV)

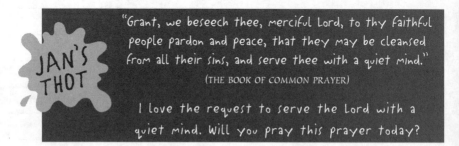

JAN'S THOT

"Grant, we beseech thee, merciful Lord, to thy faithful people pardon and peace, that they may be cleansed from all their sins, and serve thee with a quiet mind."
(THE BOOK OF COMMON PRAYER)

I love the request to serve the Lord with a quiet mind. Will you pray this prayer today?

My personal thoughts are...

_____

_____

_____

_____

_____

_____

_____

_____

_____

_____

_____

_____

Father God, today I pray for_____

_____

_____

_____

_____

_____

_____

_____

_____

_____

"For God has
not given us
a spirit of
fear, but of
power and of
love and of a
sound mind."

2 Timothy 1:7
(NKJV)

Show me Your heart about_____

_____

_____

_____

_____

_____

_____

_____

I love You for_____

_____

_____

_____

_____

_____

_____

Today's Date _____

*"Call to Me, and I will answer you, and show you great
and mighty things, which you do not know."*
JEREMIAH 33:3 (NKJV)

JAN'S THOT

Never give up—even if it looks as if things are getting worse. With God, timing is everything! We never fully know what is going on behind the scenes, so we can't gauge the outcome. The Lord simply says, "Call and I will answer." When you call upon the Lord, you'll see great and mighty things that you probably never imagined possible. What a great Father we have!

My personal thoughts are...

_____

_____

_____

_____

_____

_____

_____

_____

_____

_____

_____

_____

Heavenly Father, I call on You for my family in:

~~~~~~

I call on You to thank You for_____

~~~~~~

I call on You for my friends:

1 _____
2 _____
3 _____
4 _____
5 _____
6 _____
7 _____
8 _____
9 _____
10 _____
11 _____
12 _____
13 _____
14 _____
15 _____

*"He who keeps the commandment keeps his soul,
but he who is careless of his ways will die."*
PROVERBS 19:16 (NKJV)

JAN'S THOT

Why not list several times when you might have been a little careless in your ways? What was the result? Sweeping our indiscretions under the rug only makes the rug lumpy. It is important to do a good clean-up job when we've been careless.

My personal thoughts are...

_____
_____
_____
_____
_____
_____
_____
_____
_____
_____
_____
_____
_____

Father, I praise You for _____

~~~~~~
~~~~~~
~~~~~~
~~~~~~
~~~~~~
~~~~~~
~~~~~~
~~~~~~

I ask You to work in my life specifically in the areas where I have been careless:

~~~~~~
~~~~~~
~~~~~~
~~~~~~
~~~~~~
~~~~~~
~~~~~~
~~~~~~
~~~~~~
~~~~~~

I pray for these I love who have been careless:

1 _____
2 _____
3 _____
4 _____
5 _____
6 _____
7 _____
8 _____
9 _____
10 _____
11 _____
12 _____
13 _____
14 _____
15 _____

"And whenever you stand praying, if you have anything against anyone, forgive him, that your Father in heaven may also forgive you your trespasses."

MARK 11:25 (NKJV)

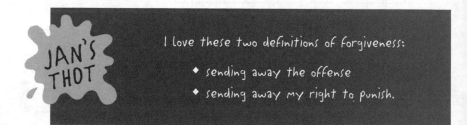

JAN'S THOT

I love these two definitions of forgiveness:

◆ sending away the offense
◆ sending away my right to punish.

Do you have your own definition of forgiveness? Has it affected the way you live your life? If so, write down how it has affected your life.

_____

_____

_____

_____

_____

_____

_____

_____

_____

Father, sometimes I struggle with forgiving people when they _____

_____

_____

_____

_____

_____

I want Your forgiveness for...

_____

_____

_____

_____

_____

_____

_____

_____

Give me grace in coming days as I face the following people who I find to be difficult:

_____

_____

_____

_____

_____

_____

_____

I know I need to forgive...

1 _____

2 _____

3 _____

4 _____

5 _____

6 _____

7 _____

8 _____

9 _____

10 _____

11 _____

12 _____

13 _____

14 _____

15 _____

"I say then; Walk in the Spirit, and you shall not fulfill the lust of the flesh."
GALATIANS 5:16 (NKJV)

When Jesus left the earth, He left the Holy Spirit behind to comfort, guide, and teach us. Because we have the Spirit of Jesus residing within us, ready to guide us in every situation, we should have confidence to face all situations—even the trying ones.

My personal thoughts are...

_____

_____

_____

_____

_____

_____

_____

_____

_____

_____

_____

_____

Blessed Father, thank You for giving me what I need to...

_____
_____
_____
_____
_____
_____
_____
_____
_____
_____
_____
_____
_____
_____
_____
_____
_____
_____

Teach me to rely on the Holy Spirit more in these areas:

_____
_____
_____
_____
_____
_____
_____
_____
_____
_____
_____
_____
_____

I pray for_____
_____
_____
_____
_____
_____
_____

"The fear of the Lord is the beginning of wisdom; a good understanding have all those who do His commandments. His praise endures forever."

PSALM 111:10 (NKJV)

JAN'S THOT

If you are confused about a decision, remember—it is God who has the answer. Believe that He is right, and you will be closer to your decision than ever before!

My personal thoughts are...

_____

_____

_____

_____

_____

_____

_____

_____

_____

_____

_____

_____

Heavenly Father, I want to be wise concerning:

_____
_____
_____
_____
_____
_____
_____
_____
_____
_____

I pray for these with whom I have a hard time:

_____
_____
_____
_____
_____
_____
_____
_____
_____
_____

I pray for these that I love:

_____
_____
_____
_____
_____
_____
_____
_____
_____
_____

I love You for...

_____
_____
_____
_____
_____
_____
_____
_____
_____
_____

Today's Date _____

"But seek first the kingdom of God and His righteousness,
and all these things shall be added to you."

MATTHEW 6:33 (NKJV)

JAN'S THOT

If you seek for something, you hunt diligently. It is not a casual look-see, but a focused search for an answer! What are you seeking from God today?

My personal thoughts are...

_____

_____

_____

_____

_____

_____

_____

_____

_____

_____

_____

_____

Lord God, My heart wants to understand what it means to "seek first the kingdom of God..."

I give You my family and their needs:_____
~~~~~~~~~~~~~~~~~~~~
~~~~~~~~~~~~~~~~~~~~
~~~~~~~~~~~~~~~~~~~~
~~~~~~~~~~~~~~~~~~~~
~~~~~~~~~~~~~~~~~~~~
~~~~~~~~~~~~~~~~~~~~
~~~~~~~~~~~~~~~~~~~~
~~~~~~~~~~~~~~~~~~~~
~~~~~~~~~~~~~~~~~~~~
~~~~~~~~~~~~~~~~~~~~

I give You my personal needs:
~~~~~~~~~~~~~~~~~~~~
~~~~~~~~~~~~~~~~~~~~
~~~~~~~~~~~~~~~~~~~~
~~~~~~~~~~~~~~~~~~~~
~~~~~~~~~~~~~~~~~~~~
~~~~~~~~~~~~~~~~~~~~
~~~~~~~~~~~~~~~~~~~~
~~~~~~~~~~~~~~~~~~~~
~~~~~~~~~~~~~~~~~~~~

I give You my friends and their needs:_____
~~~~~~~~~~~~~~~~~~~~
~~~~~~~~~~~~~~~~~~~~
~~~~~~~~~~~~~~~~~~~~
~~~~~~~~~~~~~~~~~~~~
~~~~~~~~~~~~~~~~~~~~
~~~~~~~~~~~~~~~~~~~~
~~~~~~~~~~~~~~~~~~~~
~~~~~~~~~~~~~~~~~~~~

I give You my responsibilities and what they take from me:
~~~~~~~~~~~~~~~~~~~~
~~~~~~~~~~~~~~~~~~~~
~~~~~~~~~~~~~~~~~~~~
~~~~~~~~~~~~~~~~~~~~
~~~~~~~~~~~~~~~~~~~~
~~~~~~~~~~~~~~~~~~~~
~~~~~~~~~~~~~~~~~~~~

"I will sing to the Lord all my life; I will sing praises to my God as long as I live.
May my thoughts please him; I am happy in the Lord."

PSALMS 104:33, 34 (NCV)

JAN'S THOT

God knows your thoughts before you speak them. It's
awesome to realize that even what you think is part
of your relationship with Him. What's on your mind
right now?

My personal thoughts are...

_____
_____
_____
_____
_____
_____
_____
_____
_____
_____
_____
_____

Father God, I come to You with my prayer today.

Father, I love You for . . .

_____

_____

_____

_____

_____

_____

_____

_____

_____

I ask You to teach me something I need to know today

_____

_____

_____

_____

_____

_____

_____

_____

Help me to understand my
own thoughts on . . .

_____

_____

_____

_____

_____

_____

_____

_____

_____

I ask You to take care of...

_____

_____

_____

_____

_____

_____

_____

_____

_____

"Love does not harm a neighbor. Therefore love is the fulfillment of the law."
ROMANS 13:10 (NKJV)

JAN'S THOT

List some ways you have loved your neighbors in the last six months. If you can't come up with something tangible, it might be time to actively look for ways to reach out and love those you call neighbors.

How are you loving your neighbors?

_____

_____

_____

_____

_____

_____

_____

_____

_____

_____

_____

Father, I love You for_____
_____
_____
_____
_____
_____
_____
_____

I pray You will give me a love for...

_____
_____
_____
_____
_____

I pray that You will care for...

_____
_____
_____
_____

I lift these neigh-
bors before you...

1 _____
2 _____
3 _____
4 _____
5 _____
6 _____
7 _____
8 _____
9 _____
10 _____
11 _____
12 _____
13 _____
14 _____
15 _____

I praise You for

_____
_____
_____
_____

"Get rid of all bitterness, rage and anger, brawling and slander,
along with every form of malice. Be kind and compassionate to one another,
forgiving each other, just as in Christ God forgave you."

EPHESIANS 4:31, 32 (NIV)

JAN'S THOT

If you died tonight, what would the people you love remember about you? Kindness, tender-heartedness, and forgiveness should be the characteristics for which you're to be remembered.

My personal thoughts are...

_____

_____

_____

_____

_____

_____

_____

_____

_____

_____

_____

_____

Father, thank You for Your kindness to me in:

~~~~~~~~~~~~~~~~~~~~~~~~~~~~~~~~~~~
~~~~~~~~~~~~~~~~~~~~~~~~~~~~~~~~~~~
~~~~~~~~~~~~~~~~~~~~~~~~~~~~~~~~~~~
~~~~~~~~~~~~~~~~~~~~~~~~~~~~~~~~~~~
~~~~~~~~~~~~~~~~~~~~~~~~~~~~~~~~~~~

I ask You to show me how to extend Your kindness to...

1 _____
2 _____
3 _____
4 _____
5 _____
6 _____
7 _____
8 _____
9 _____
10 _____
11 _____
12 _____
13 _____
14 _____
15 _____

Thank You for Your kindness to my family in:

~~~~~~~~~~~~~~~~~~~~~~~~~~~~~~~~~~~
~~~~~~~~~~~~~~~~~~~~~~~~~~~~~~~~~~~
~~~~~~~~~~~~~~~~~~~~~~~~~~~~~~~~~~~
~~~~~~~~~~~~~~~~~~~~~~~~~~~~~~~~~~~
~~~~~~~~~~~~~~~~~~~~~~~~~~~~~~~~~~~
~~~~~~~~~~~~~~~~~~~~~~~~~~~~~~~~~~~

I love You for _____
~~~~~~~~~~~~~~~~~~~~~~~~~~~~~~~~~~~
~~~~~~~~~~~~~~~~~~~~~~~~~~~~~~~~~~~
~~~~~~~~~~~~~~~~~~~~~~~~~~~~~~~~~~~
~~~~~~~~~~~~~~~~~~~~~~~~~~~~~~~~~~~
~~~~~~~~~~~~~~~~~~~~~~~~~~~~~~~~~~~
~~~~~~~~~~~~~~~~~~~~~~~~~~~~~~~~~~~

"These things I have spoken to you, that in Me you may have peace. In the world you will have tribulation' but be of good cheer, I have overcome the world."

JOHN 16:33 (NKJV)

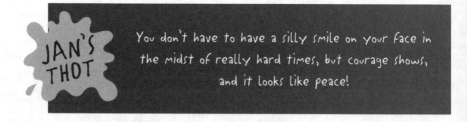

JAN'S THOT

You don't have to have a silly smile on your face in the midst of really hard times, but courage shows, and it looks like peace!

My personal thoughts are...

_____

_____

_____

_____

_____

_____

_____

_____

_____

_____

_____

_____

_____

Father, I want to learn to have peace and be of good cheer in everything.

Teach me how to see Your side of these situations:

_____
_____
_____
_____
_____
_____
_____
_____
_____
_____
_____
_____
_____
_____
_____
_____
_____
_____
_____
_____

I ask You to show me how to extend Your kindness to...

1 _____
2 _____
3 _____
4 _____
5 _____
6 _____
7 _____
8 _____

I love You for_____
_____
_____
_____
_____
_____
_____
_____
_____
_____
_____
_____
_____
_____

"O You who hear prayer; to You all flesh will come."
PSALM 65:2 (NKJV)

JAN'S THOT

Someday all flesh will bow before the Lord and acknowledge who He is—but for now, we can bow before Him in prayer and know that He hears us. There is a big difference between simply acknowledging God's sovereignty and actually worshiping Him.

My personal thoughts are...

_____
_____
_____
_____
_____
_____
_____
_____
_____
_____
_____
_____
_____

Father, forgive me for failing to trust
Your ability in...

_____

_____

_____

_____

_____

_____

_____

_____

I love You for _____

_____

_____

_____

_____

_____

_____

_____

_____

_____

_____

_____

I ask You to work in
the lives of these
people...

1 _____

2 _____

3 _____

4 _____

5 _____

6 _____

7 _____

8 _____

9 _____

10 _____

11 _____

12 _____

13 _____

14 _____

15 _____

"When you pass through the waters, I will be with you; and through the rivers, they shall not overflow you. When you walk through the fire, you shall not be burned, nor shall the flame scorch you."

ISAIAH 43:2 (NKJV)

JAN'S THOT

When you pass through the waters and walk through the flames, your eyes are on the deepness and the heat. That is the normal human response to extreme pressure. But you can be comforted with the fact that God's eyes are on you. He isn't worried about the waves or the fire—His concern is for you!

My personal thoughts are...

_____
_____
_____
_____
_____
_____
_____
_____
_____
_____
_____
_____
_____
_____

Father God, I come to You with my prayer today.

Father, I want to know that
You are with me in...

_____

_____

_____

_____

_____

_____

_____

_____

I look to You to answer my
questions about_____

_____

_____

_____

_____

_____

_____

_____

_____

_____

I long to know that You have
the following people or issues
in your care:

_____

_____

_____

_____

_____

_____

_____

_____

I love You for_____

_____

_____

_____

_____

_____

_____

_____

_____

"Long ago God spoke in many different ways to our fathers through the prophets, in visions, dreams, and even face-to-face, telling them little by little about his plans. But now in these days he has spoken to us through his Son to whom he has given everything and through whom he made the world and everything there is."

HEBREWS 1:1, 2 (TLB)

JAN'S THOT

When God sent Jesus Christ, that was His Final Word. We will no longer see prophets, nor prophetic words from Heaven. Today, if you want to know God, you have to come through the Son. Christ summed up the totality of His redemptive work with three poignant words: "It is Finished!"

My personal thoughts are...

_____
_____
_____
_____
_____
_____
_____
_____
_____
_____
_____
_____

Lord God, I want to know the person of Jesus Christ more intimately in my life.

Help me to understand His purpose for me as it relates to _____

_____
_____
_____
_____
_____
_____
_____
_____
_____
_____

I love You for _____

_____
_____
_____
_____
_____
_____
_____
_____
_____
_____
_____

I want to know_____

_____
_____
_____
_____
_____
_____
_____
_____
_____
_____
_____

I pray for _____

_____
_____
_____
_____
_____
_____
_____
_____
_____
_____
_____

Today's Date _____

"His name shall endure forever; His name shall continue as long as the sun. And men shall be blessed in Him; all nations shall call Him blessed."

PSALM 72:17 (NKJV)

JAN'S THOT

I love the verse that says, "IN YOUR DISTRESS YOU CALLED AND I RESCUED YOU, I ANSWERED YOU OUT OF A THUNDERCLOUD" (Psalm 81:7). When we call, we are calling on the Name that endures forever. So whether it is in thunderclouds, in sunny weather, or when the stars are the only light we have, His name is there.

My personal thoughts are...

_____

_____

_____

_____

_____

_____

_____

_____

_____

_____

_____

_____

Father, I thank You for sending me life in Jesus Christ, the name above every name!

_____
_____
_____
_____
_____
_____
_____
_____

I love You for_____
_____
_____
_____
_____
_____
_____

I pray for_____
_____
_____
_____
_____
_____

Father, I pray that You would bring the following people into a relationship with your Son:

1 _____
2 _____
3 _____
4 _____
5 _____
6 _____
7 _____
8 _____
9 _____
10 _____
11 _____
12 _____
13 _____
14 _____

Surprise!!!!!

What is your favorite song right now? For what reason?

_____

_____

_____

_____

_____

What has God whispered in your ear lately through a song, a poem, or a CD? Could you write what He has whispered? (Don't be ashamed. Just write it out and be amazed at His love.)

_____

_____

_____

_____

_____

_____

What are the whispers of your heart to Him? Could you write your whispers to Him and read them out loud? (I think you might be surprised at the sweetness of the moment!)

_____

_____

_____

_____

_____

_____

_____

_____

_____

_____

You are His Beloved......

"My beloved said to me, 'Rise up, my love, my fair one, and come away. For the winter is past, the rain is over and gone. The flowers are springing up and the time of the singing of birds has come. Yes, spring is here...My beloved is mine and I am his . . .' "

SONG OF SOLOMON 2:10–12, 16 (LB)

*"So do not throw away your confidence; it will be richly rewarded.
You need to persevere so that when you have done the will of God,
you will receive what He has promised."*

HEBREWS 10:35, 36 (NIV)

JAN'S THOT

"Thank God! a man can grow!
He is not bound
With earthward gaze to creep along the ground:
Though his beginnings be but poor and low,
Thank God a man can grow!"

(AUTHOR UNKNOWN)

My personal thoughts are...

_____
_____
_____
_____
_____
_____
_____
_____
_____
_____
_____
_____
_____

Father God, I want to grow in these
areas of my life:

_____

_____

_____

_____

_____

_____

_____

I thank You that I have grown in these
areas:

_____

_____

_____

_____

_____

_____

I love You for_____

_____

_____

_____

_____

_____

_____

_____

I ask You to work in
the lives of...

1 _____

2 _____

3 _____

4 _____

5 _____

6 _____

7 _____

8 _____

9 _____

10 _____

11 _____

12 _____

13 _____

14 _____

15 _____

"I press toward the
goal for the prize
of the upward call
of God in Christ
Jesus."

Philippians 3:14

*"The wise woman builds her house, but with her own hands
the foolish one tears hers down."*

PROVERBS 14:1 (NIV)

JAN'S THOT

Building a house requires many skills—sacrifice,
wisdom, laughter, and prayer. It's amazing what a
woman can do with these four traits.

My personal thoughts are...

_____
_____
_____
_____
_____
_____
_____
_____
_____
_____
_____
_____
_____
_____
_____

Father God, I come to You with my prayer today.

Father, I pray that You might make me a better woman in these areas:

_____
_____
_____
_____
_____
_____
_____
_____
_____
_____

I pray for my family (immediate and/or extended):

_____
_____
_____
_____
_____
_____
_____
_____
_____
_____

Thank You for what You have done in me in regard to...

_____
_____
_____
_____
_____
_____
_____
_____

I love You for_____

_____
_____
_____
_____
_____
_____
_____
_____
_____
_____

"This is what the Lord says: 'Let not the wise man boast of his wisdom or the strong man boast of his strength or the rich man boast of his riches, but let him who boasts, boast about this: that he understands and knows me, that I am the Lord, who exercises kindness, justice and righteousness on earth, for in these I delight.'"

JEREMIAH 9:23, 24 (NIV)

JAN'S THOT

In what are you boasting? Is it who you know? Where you've excelled? What you own? What you've achieved? Or where you live? If so, you may want to back up and think about Who has brought you here, and why you are blessed beyond measure.

My personal thoughts are...

_____

_____

_____

_____

_____

_____

_____

_____

_____

_____

_____

_____

Father God, I come to You with my prayer today.

Lord God, I bow before You
and thank You for...

_____
_____
_____
_____
_____
_____
_____
_____
_____
_____

I ask mercy for_____
_____
_____
_____
_____
_____
_____
_____
_____
_____
_____
_____
_____

I ask You to work in my spirit
to _____
_____
_____
_____
_____
_____
_____
_____
_____
_____
_____

I love You for_____
_____
_____
_____
_____
_____
_____
_____
_____
_____
_____
_____

"He who walks with the wise grows wise, but a companion of fools suffers harm."
PROVERBS 13:20 (NIV)

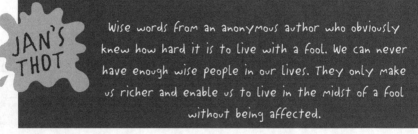

"THOSE WHO ADMIRE STRENGTH IN A RASCAL DO NOT LIVE IN HIS TOWN."

JAN'S THOT

Wise words from an anonymous author who obviously knew how hard it is to live with a fool. We can never have enough wise people in our lives. They only make us richer and enable us to live in the midst of a fool without being affected.

My personal thoughts are...

_____

_____

_____

_____

_____

_____

_____

_____

_____

_____

_____

_____

Lord God, I thank You that You have shown me...

_____

_____

_____

_____

_____

_____

_____

_____

_____

_____

_____

I love You for _____

_____

_____

_____

_____

_____

_____

_____

_____

_____

I pray for wisdom in my relationships with...

1 _____

2 _____

3 _____

4 _____

5 _____

6 _____

7 _____

8 _____

9 _____

10 _____

11 _____

12 _____

13 _____

14 _____

15 _____

*"In the morning, O Lord, you hear my voice; in the morning
I lay my requests before you and wait in expectation."*

PSALM 5:3 (NIV)

JAN'S THOT

I love the Lord because there are no eggshells around
His throne. I can run right into His presence without
fear or intimidation. What a gift!

My personal thoughts are...

_____

_____

_____

_____

_____

_____

_____

_____

_____

_____

_____

_____

_____

_____

father, thank You for a new day.

I pray for this difficulty:

_____

_____

_____

_____

_____

_____

_____

I love You for_____

_____

_____

_____

_____

_____

_____

I pray today for
my family and
friends:

1 _____

2 _____

3 _____

4 _____

5 _____

6 _____

7 _____

8 _____

9 _____

10 _____

11 _____

12 _____

13 _____

14 _____

15 _____

"So, let us know; let us press on to know the Lord. His going forth is as certain as the dawn; And He will come to us like the rain, Like the spring rain watering the earth."

HOSEA 6:3 (NASB)

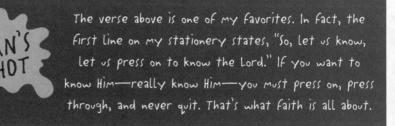

JAN'S THOT

The verse above is one of my favorites. In fact, the first line on my stationery states, "So, let us know, let us press on to know the Lord." If you want to know Him—really know Him—you must press on, press through, and never quit. That's what faith is all about.

My personal thoughts are...

_____
_____
_____
_____
_____
_____
_____
_____
_____
_____
_____
_____
_____

Lord, I thank You for my life and for letting me know You. I want to know You better in these areas:

_____
_____
_____
_____
_____
_____

I ask you to_____
_____
_____
_____
_____
_____

I love You for_____
_____
_____
_____
_____
_____
_____
_____
_____

I ask You to work as only You can in the lives of the following people:

1 _____
2 _____
3 _____
4 _____
5 _____
6 _____
7 _____
8 _____
9 _____
10 _____
11 _____
12 _____
13 _____
14 _____
15 _____

"The memory of the righteous will be a blessing, but the name of the wicked will rot."
PROVERBS 10:7 (NIV)

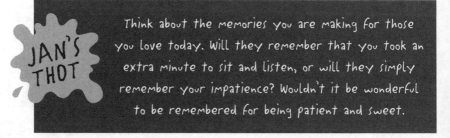

JAN'S THOT

Think about the memories you are making for those you love today. Will they remember that you took an extra minute to sit and listen, or will they simply remember your impatience? Wouldn't it be wonderful to be remembered for being patient and sweet.

My personal thoughts are...

_____
_____
_____
_____
_____
_____
_____
_____
_____
_____
_____
_____
_____

Father, I want my memory to be a blessing.
I want my life to bring relief not grief.

Show me what might be
blocking the blessing.

_____
_____
_____
_____
_____
_____
_____

Show me what will be a blessing.

_____
_____
_____
_____
_____
_____
_____

Thank You for loving me in
these ways:

_____
_____
_____
_____
_____
_____
_____
_____
_____
_____

I pray for

_____

who is someone I need to learn
to bless.

"If it is possible, as far as it depends on you, live at peace with everyone."
ROMANS 12:18 (NIV)

JAN'S THOT

I love the statement in Proverbs that says, "A man's discretion makes him slow to anger, And it is his glory to overlook a transgression" (Proverbs 19:11 NASB) Why don't you see what you can overlook today?

My personal thoughts are...

_____

_____

_____

_____

_____

_____

_____

_____

_____

_____

_____

_____

_____

Abba-father, I praise You for giving me peace through Your son, Jesus Christ. Since I have been in Him and He in me, I have found peace in these areas:

_____
_____
_____
_____
_____
_____
_____
_____
_____

I love You for

_____
_____
_____
_____
_____
_____
_____
_____
_____
_____

I pray that the following people will come to know You and find peace:

1 _____
2 _____
3 _____
4 _____
5 _____
6 _____
7 _____
8 _____
9 _____
10 _____
11 _____
12 _____
13 _____
14 _____
15 _____

"May the LORD reward your work, and your wages be full from the LORD,
the God of Israel, under whose wings you have come to seek refuge."

RUTH 2:12 (NASB)

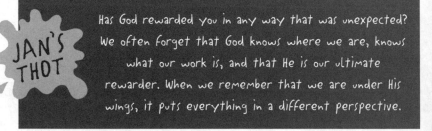

JAN'S THOT

Has God rewarded you in any way that was unexpected? We often forget that God knows where we are, knows what our work is, and that He is our ultimate rewarder. When we remember that we are under His wings, it puts everything in a different perspective.

My personal thoughts are...

_____
_____
_____
_____
_____
_____
_____
_____
_____
_____
_____
_____
_____

Father, thank You for loving me. I want to love_____
more, and I want to love this person or these people with real sincerity. When I have taken refuge in You, I have discovered...

_____
_____
_____
_____
_____
_____
_____
_____

I love You for _____

_____
_____
_____
_____
_____
_____
_____
_____
_____
_____

My goals for the next few days...

_____
_____
_____
_____
_____
_____
_____
_____
_____
_____
_____
_____
_____
_____
_____
_____

"I will be your God throughout your lifetime—until your hair is white with age. I made you, and I will care for you. I will carry you along and save you."

ISAIAH 46:4 (NLT)

JAN'S THOT

It's a stunning thought to realize that God has always had you on his mind. Even when you don't give God a fleeting thought, He is acutely aware of you; He has His hand on you and will keep His hand upon you until you reach home!

My personal thoughts are...

_____

_____

_____

_____

_____

_____

_____

_____

_____

_____

_____

_____

Father, I don't know exactly
when I was first aware of You
but I think it may have been...

_____
_____
_____
_____
_____
_____
_____
_____
_____
_____

I pray that You will work in
my life regarding...

_____
_____
_____
_____
_____
_____
_____
_____
_____
_____
_____

Thank You for keeping me on
Your mind even when I...

_____
_____
_____
_____
_____
_____
_____
_____
_____
_____

I love You for_____

_____
_____
_____
_____
_____
_____
_____
_____
_____
_____
_____

Today's Date _____

"Let those who want to do wrong stay away from me; I will have nothing to do with evil. If anyone secretly says things against his neighbor, I will stop him. I will not allow people to be proud and look down on others."

PSALMS 101:4, 5 (NCV)

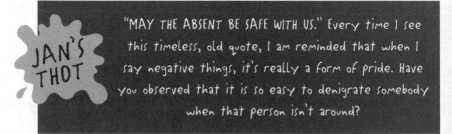

JAN'S THOT

"MAY THE ABSENT BE SAFE WITH US." Every time I see this timeless, old quote, I am reminded that when I say negative things, it's really a form of pride. Have you observed that it is so easy to denigrate somebody when that person isn't around?

My personal thoughts are...

_____
_____
_____
_____
_____
_____
_____
_____
_____
_____
_____
_____
_____

Father God, I want to be free of any
kind of critical spirit. Show me where I
am critical.

_____
_____
_____
_____
_____
_____
_____
_____
_____
_____
_____

I love You for loving me when I...

_____
_____
_____
_____
_____
_____
_____
_____
_____
_____
_____

I choose to pray
for those I've criti-
cized in the past:

1 _____
2 _____
3 _____
4 _____
5 _____
6 _____
7 _____
8 _____
9 _____
10 _____
11 _____
12 _____
13 _____
14 _____
15 _____

"But no man can
tame the tongue. It
is an unruly evil, full
of deadly poison."

James 3:8

"Give instruction to a wise man, and he will be still wiser, Teach a righteous man, and he will increase his learning. The fear of the LORD is the beginning of wisdom, And the knowledge of the Holy One is understanding."

PROVERBS 9:9, 10 (NASB)

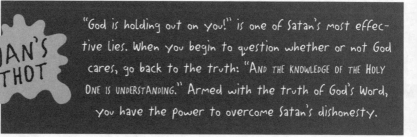

JAN'S THOT

"God is holding out on you!" is one of Satan's most effective lies. When you begin to question whether or not God cares, go back to the truth: "AND THE KNOWLEDGE OF THE HOLY ONE IS UNDERSTANDING." Armed with the truth of God's Word, you have the power to overcome Satan's dishonesty.

My personal thoughts are...

_____

_____

_____

_____

_____

_____

_____

_____

_____

_____

_____

_____

Father God, I thank You for being the Holy One.
I acknowledge that You are all wise.
I want to be a wise woman in a very unwise world.

I need Your insight about...

_____
_____
_____
_____
_____
_____
_____
_____
_____
_____

I love You for loving me and for_____

_____
_____
_____
_____
_____
_____
_____
_____

I ask You to open my eyes to my own faults.

_____
_____
_____
_____
_____
_____
_____
_____

I ask forgiveness for...

_____
_____
_____
_____
_____
_____
_____

"If someone says, 'I love God,' and hates his brother, he is a liar; for the one who does not love his brother whom he has seen, cannot love God whom he has not seen. And this commandment we have from Him, that the one who loves God should love his brother also."

1 JOHN 4:20, 21 (NASB)

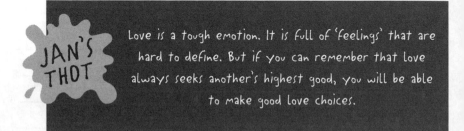

JAN'S THOT

Love is a tough emotion. It is full of 'feelings' that are hard to define. But if you can remember that love always seeks another's highest good, you will be able to make good love choices.

My personal thoughts are...

_____
_____
_____
_____
_____
_____
_____
_____
_____
_____
_____
_____
_____

Father, thank You for loving me and for always seeking my highest good. Help me to know and to choose the highest good for _____

_____

_____

_____

_____

_____

_____

_____

I love You.

Would You show me Your highest good?

_____

_____

_____

_____

_____

_____

I lift these people before you...

1 _____

2 _____

3 _____

4 _____

5 _____

6 _____

7 _____

8 _____

9 _____

10 _____

11 _____

12 _____

13 _____

14 _____

15 _____

"And blessed is she who believed that there would be a fulfillment
of what had been spoken to her by the Lord."

LUKE 1:45 (NASB)

JAN'S THOT

Has the Lord spoken to you about anything? Do you
dare share what was communicated to you? When God
speaks, He wants you to take Him at His Word. He
wants you to believe. What has the Lord spoken to
you about recently?

_____

_____

_____

_____

_____

_____

_____

_____

_____

_____

_____

_____

_____

Father God, help me to
believe You about...

_____
_____
_____
_____
_____
_____
_____
_____
_____
_____

Would You confirm Your will to
me through Your Word?

_____
_____
_____
_____
_____
_____
_____
_____
_____
_____

I think I heard You say...

_____
_____
_____
_____
_____
_____
_____
_____
_____
_____
_____
_____
_____

I love You for_____

_____
_____
_____
_____
_____
_____
_____
_____
_____
_____
_____
_____
_____

Today's Date _____

"Teach me Thy way, O LORD, And lead me in a level path, Because of my foes."
PSALMS 27:11 (NASB)

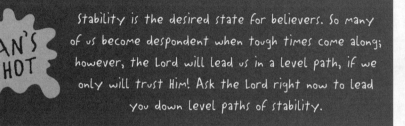

JAN'S THOT

Stability is the desired state for believers. So many of us become despondent when tough times come along; however, the Lord will lead us in a level path, if we only will trust Him! Ask the Lord right now to lead you down level paths of stability.

My personal thoughts are...

_____
_____
_____
_____
_____
_____
_____
_____
_____
_____
_____
_____
_____

Father God, I come to You with my prayer today.

Heavenly Father, I want to honor You with my feelings regarding_____

_____
_____
_____
_____
_____
_____
_____
_____

I pray that You will...

_____
_____
_____
_____
_____
_____
_____
_____
_____
_____

Show me how to walk in a level path when I think of...

_____
_____
_____
_____
_____
_____
_____
_____
_____

I love You for_____

_____
_____
_____
_____
_____
_____
_____
_____
_____

Today's Date _____

"For nothing will be impossible with God."
LUKE 1:37 (NASB)

JAN'S THOT

No matter how impossible things look to you, God's ability does not rest on what you can see but on who He is. Are you burdened with circumstances that seem impossible to resolve?

My personal thoughts on my circumstances are...

_____

_____

_____

_____

_____

_____

_____

_____

_____

_____

_____

_____

_____

Why not pray the following prayer and lay all these burdens at God's throne?

O Father, I look to You as the only One who can do the impossible. I see the following situations as impossible apart from You: _____

_____

_____

_____

_____

_____

_____

_____

I ask You to do what only You can do in each situation. I thank You for doing the impossible. I love You for...

_____

_____

_____

_____

_____

_____

_____

_____

_____

_____

I lift these people before you...

1 _____

2 _____

3 _____

4 _____

5 _____

6 _____

7 _____

8 _____

9 _____

10 _____

11 _____

12 _____

13 _____

14 _____

15 _____

Today's Date _____

"Happy are those who don't listen to the wicked, who don't go where sinners go, who don't do what evil people do. They love the Lord's teachings, and they think about those teachings day and night."

PSALMS 1:1, 2 (NCV)

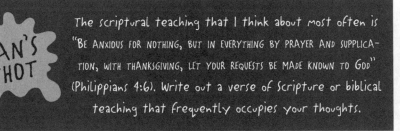

JAN'S THOT

The scriptural teaching that I think about most often is "BE ANXIOUS FOR NOTHING, BUT IN EVERYTHING BY PRAYER AND SUPPLICATION, WITH THANKSGIVING, LET YOUR REQUESTS BE MADE KNOWN TO GOD" (Philippians 4:6). Write out a verse of Scripture or biblical teaching that frequently occupies your thoughts.

My personal thoughts are...

_____

_____

_____

_____

_____

_____

_____

_____

_____

_____

_____

_____

Father God, I come to You with my prayer today.

Father, sometimes I have trouble believing_____

_____

_____

_____

_____

_____

_____

_____

_____

_____

I ask You to bless...

_____

_____

_____

_____

_____

_____

_____

_____

_____

_____

_____

I thank You for what You have done even when I don't believe.

_____

_____

_____

_____

_____

_____

_____

_____

_____

I love You for_____

_____

_____

_____

_____

_____

_____

_____

_____

_____

"I have heard of Thee by the hearing of the ear; But now my eye sees Thee."
JOB 42:5 (NASB)

JAN'S THOT

Experiencing God is not just a factual knowledge of who God is—it is a sensory experience. When you experience God, you literally see God at work in your life and feel his presence!

What are some ways you are sensing God's presence in your life?

_____

_____

_____

_____

_____

_____

_____

_____

_____

_____

_____

Holy Father, I want to know You in a way
that cannot be taken away from me.

You have shown Yourself in
the past by_____

_____
_____
_____
_____
_____
_____
_____
_____
_____
_____
_____
_____
_____
_____
_____
_____
_____
_____

I ask You to show Yourself now
in the following situations:

_____
_____
_____
_____
_____
_____
_____
_____
_____
_____
_____
_____

I thank You that You are able
to...

_____
_____
_____
_____
_____
_____

"Though a host encamp against me, My heart will not fear; Though war arise against me, In spite of this I shall be confident. One thing I have asked from the LORD, that I shall seek: That I may dwell in the house of the LORD all the days of my life, To behold the beauty of the LORD, And to meditate in His temple."

PSALMS 27:3, 4 (NASB)

JAN'S THOT

If you have ever felt as if a 'host were camping against you,' you know the courage it takes not to fear! To believe that the Lord is in control of any circumstance takes supreme confidence, and confidence is a choice in the face of hard facts. Remember, God is on your side, no matter how menacing the enemy looks!

Do you feel as if a host were camping against you today?

_____

_____

_____

_____

_____

_____

_____

_____

_____

_____

_____

Father God, I choose to believe You today about:

_____

_____

_____

_____

_____

_____

_____

I pray for_____

_____

_____

_____

_____

I ask you to do what only You can do. I love You for _____

_____

_____

_____

_____

_____

_____

Recent answers to prayer:

_____

_____

_____

_____

_____

_____

_____

_____

_____

_____

_____

_____

_____

_____

_____

_____

"It is better to take refuge in the LORD than to trust in man. It is better to take refuge in the LORD than to trust in princes."

PSALMS 118:8, 9 (NASB)

JAN'S THOT

We can become confused when we let those we love be our saviors or when we ourselves attempt to fix things that only God can redeem! There is but one Savior. Are you trying to resolve conflicts or dilemmas in your life that only God can resolve?

My personal thoughts are...

_____

_____

_____

_____

_____

_____

_____

_____

_____

_____

_____

_____

Lord God, forgive me for trying to fix

_____

_____

_____

_____

_____

_____

_____

forgive me for turning my hope toward

_____

_____

_____

instead of to You.

I love You for_____

_____

_____

_____

_____

_____

_____

_____

_____

I lift these needs
before you...

_____

_____

_____

_____

_____

_____

_____

_____

_____

_____

_____

_____

_____

_____

_____

_____

"The wicked flee when no one is pursuing, But the righteous are bold as a lion."
PROVERBS 28:1 (NASB)

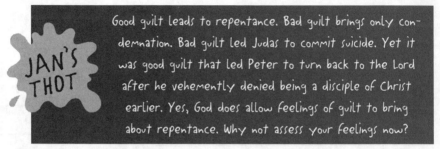

JAN'S THOT

Good guilt leads to repentance. Bad guilt brings only condemnation. Bad guilt led Judas to commit suicide. Yet it was good guilt that led Peter to turn back to the Lord after he vehemently denied being a disciple of Christ earlier. Yes, God does allow feelings of guilt to bring about repentance. Why not assess your feelings now?

My personal thoughts are...

_____

_____

_____

_____

_____

_____

_____

_____

_____

_____

_____

_____

Father, sometimes I feel guilty about...

_____
_____
_____
_____
_____
_____
_____
_____
_____

I want to be "bold as a lion" as Your Word describes. Would You show me how to feel forgiven about...

_____
_____
_____
_____
_____
_____
_____
_____

I have confessed and asked forgiveness, yet I still feel:

_____
_____
_____
_____
_____
_____
_____
_____
_____
_____

I love You for_____

_____
_____
_____
_____
_____
_____
_____
_____
_____
_____
_____

"Pride only leads to arguments, but those who take advice are wise."
PROVERBS 13:10 (NCV)

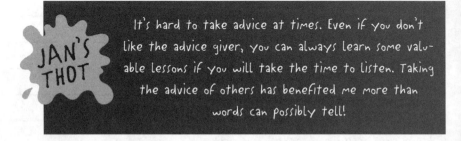

JAN'S THOT

It's hard to take advice at times. Even if you don't like the advice giver, you can always learn some valuable lessons if you will take the time to listen. Taking the advice of others has benefited me more than words can possibly tell!

Have you received some godly counsel lately?

_____
_____
_____
_____
_____

How have you responded to such advice?_____

_____
_____
_____
_____
_____

Father God, I love you for Your goodness.

_____
_____
_____
_____

I want to have ears to listen to Your advice. I pray for:

_____
_____
_____
_____
_____
_____
_____
_____
_____

I confess_____
_____
_____
_____
_____
_____
_____
_____
_____
_____

Please open the door for me to speak to...

1 _____
2 _____
3 _____
4 _____
5 _____
6 _____
7 _____
8 _____
9 _____
10 _____
11 _____
12 _____
13 _____
14 _____
15 _____

Today's Date _____

"O satisfy us in the morning with Thy lovingkindness, That we may sing for joy and be glad all our days. Make us glad according to the days Thou hast afflicted us, And the years we have seen evil."

PSALM 90:14, 15 (NASB)

JAN'S THOT

Lovingkindness is a covenant term. It notes God's love for us that has no conditions, no bounds, no rules, and no regulations. It's a love without comparison.

Describe your thoughts on lovingkindness.

_____

_____

_____

_____

_____

_____

_____

_____

_____

_____

_____

Father God, thank You for Your loving-kindness.

You have given me...

~~~~~~~~~~~~~~~~~~~~
~~~~~~~~~~~~~~~~~~~~
~~~~~~~~~~~~~~~~~~~~
~~~~~~~~~~~~~~~~~~~~
~~~~~~~~~~~~~~~~~~~~
~~~~~~~~~~~~~~~~~~~~
~~~~~~~~~~~~~~~~~~~~
~~~~~~~~~~~~~~~~~~~~
~~~~~~~~~~~~~~~~~~~~

You have made me glad about...

~~~~~~~~~~~~~~~~~~~~
~~~~~~~~~~~~~~~~~~~~
~~~~~~~~~~~~~~~~~~~~
~~~~~~~~~~~~~~~~~~~~
~~~~~~~~~~~~~~~~~~~~
~~~~~~~~~~~~~~~~~~~~
~~~~~~~~~~~~~~~~~~~~
~~~~~~~~~~~~~~~~~~~~
~~~~~~~~~~~~~~~~~~~~

I thank You for_____

~~~~~~~~~~~~~~~~~~~~
~~~~~~~~~~~~~~~~~~~~
~~~~~~~~~~~~~~~~~~~~
~~~~~~~~~~~~~~~~~~~~
~~~~~~~~~~~~~~~~~~~~
~~~~~~~~~~~~~~~~~~~~
~~~~~~~~~~~~~~~~~~~~
~~~~~~~~~~~~~~~~~~~~
~~~~~~~~~~~~~~~~~~~~
~~~~~~~~~~~~~~~~~~~~

I love You for _____

~~~~~~~~~~~~~~~~~~~~
~~~~~~~~~~~~~~~~~~~~
~~~~~~~~~~~~~~~~~~~~
~~~~~~~~~~~~~~~~~~~~
~~~~~~~~~~~~~~~~~~~~
~~~~~~~~~~~~~~~~~~~~
~~~~~~~~~~~~~~~~~~~~
~~~~~~~~~~~~~~~~~~~~
~~~~~~~~~~~~~~~~~~~~
~~~~~~~~~~~~~~~~~~~~

Sing to him; sing praises to him. Tell about all his miracles. Be glad that you are his; let those who seek the Lord be happy. Depend on the Lord and his strength; always go to him for help. Remember the miracles he has done; remember his wonders and his decisions."

PSALMS 105:2–5 (NCV)

JAN'S THOT

Can you describe a miraculous situation where God intervened on your behalf? What was the outcome for you personally? How did it affect your view of God?

Father—God, I want to sing praises to You. I love You for what You have done in my life concerning _____

_____

_____

_____

_____

_____

_____

_____

_____

_____

_____

I pray for_____

_____

_____

_____

_____

_____

_____

_____

_____

_____

_____

_____

My favorite praise songs are...

1 _____

2 _____

3 _____

4 _____

5 _____

6 _____

7 _____

8 _____

9 _____

10 _____

11 _____

12 _____

13 _____

14 _____

15 _____

Today's Date _____

He will cover you with his feathers, and under his wings you will find refuge; his faithfulness will be your shield and rampart.

PSALMS 91:4 (NIV)

JAN'S THOT

The concept of wings in this verse is a picture of protection. It is amazing how a great bird can cover her little ones with her wings so well that no one (especially predators) will know they are there. That's the beauty of being protected by the Father's wings. What a comfort it is to know that God is our "shield and rampart."

My personal thoughts are...

_____

_____

_____

_____

_____

_____

_____

_____

_____

_____

_____

_____

_____

Father God, I come to You with these burdens:

_____
_____
_____
_____
_____
_____
_____

I ask You to _____
_____
_____
_____
_____
_____
_____
_____
_____

I pray for these loved ones...

1 _____
2 _____
3 _____
4 _____
5 _____
6 _____
7 _____
8 _____
9 _____
10 _____
11 _____
12 _____
13 _____
14 _____
15 _____

I love You for _____
_____
_____
_____
_____
_____
_____

Surprise!!!!!

Who has been God's messenger to you recently?

_____

_____

_____

_____

This would be a great day to tell him/her thanks. Make a call, send a note, and ask God to bless His messenger! You might want to record the kindness of the messenger so you can remember it in the days ahead.

_____

_____

_____

_____

_____

_____

_____

_____

A word of encouragement . . . each day is a new opportunity to reclaim lost territory. If you have been "planning" to do something, why not make today the day you do it! There is nothing like accomplishing a "put off" task to feel good about yourself!

What I've done today that feels really good?

_____
_____
_____
_____
_____
_____
_____
_____
_____
_____
_____
_____
_____
_____
_____
_____
_____
_____

Things I have been planning to do for awhile...

_____
_____
_____
_____
_____
_____
_____
_____
_____
_____
_____
_____
_____
_____
_____
_____
_____
_____
_____
_____
_____
_____

"When I am afraid, I will trust in you."
PSALM 56:3 (NIV)

JAN'S THOT

When I was a little girl, I was often afraid of who might be hiding under the bed. This fear made me hesitant to go to bed. My mother taught me to say, "When I am afraid, I will put my trust in you." That almost became a litany I would repeat over and over. As an adult, I still remember what I am to do when I am afraid—put my trust in Him!

What do you do when you are afraid?

_____

_____

_____

_____

_____

_____

_____

_____

_____

_____

_____

_____

_____

Lord God, I sometimes am afraid of...

_____
_____
_____
_____
_____
_____
_____

I trust You to_____

_____
_____
_____
_____

_____

I love You for...

_____
_____
_____
_____
_____
_____
_____

I lift these people before you...

1 _____
2 _____
3 _____
4 _____
5 _____
6 _____
7 _____
8 _____
9 _____
10 _____
11 _____
12 _____
13 _____
14 _____
15 _____

"But let all those
rejoice who put
their trust in You."

Psalm 5:11

Today's Date _____

"Blessed is he whose transgression is forgiven, whose sin is covered....I acknowledged my sin to You, and my iniquity I have not hidden. I said, 'I will confess my transgressions to the Lord,' and You forgave the iniquity of my sin."

PSALM 32:1, 5 (NKJV)

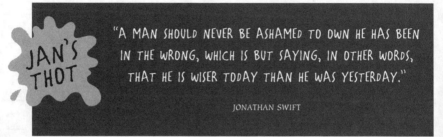

JAN'S THOT

"A MAN SHOULD NEVER BE ASHAMED TO OWN HE HAS BEEN IN THE WRONG, WHICH IS BUT SAYING, IN OTHER WORDS, THAT HE IS WISER TODAY THAN HE WAS YESTERDAY."

JONATHAN SWIFT

My personal thoughts are...

_____

_____

_____

_____

_____

_____

_____

_____

_____

_____

_____

_____

_____

Father God, I praise You for...

_____
_____
_____
_____
_____
_____
_____

I thank You for
saving me from...

_____
_____
_____
_____
_____
_____
_____
_____
_____
_____
_____
_____
_____

I ask You to work in
the lives of...

1 _____
2 _____
3 _____
4 _____
5 _____
6 _____
7 _____
8 _____
9 _____
10 _____
11 _____
12 _____
13 _____
14 _____
15 _____
16 _____
17 _____
18 _____
19 _____
20 _____
21 _____
22 _____

"A man's own folly ruins his life, yet his heart rages against the LORD."
PROVERBS 19:3 (NIV)

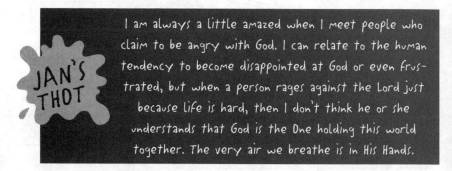

JAN'S THOT

I am always a little amazed when I meet people who claim to be angry with God. I can relate to the human tendency to become disappointed at God or even frustrated, but when a person rages against the Lord just because life is hard, then I don't think he or she understands that God is the One holding this world together. The very air we breathe is in His Hands.

My personal thoughts are...

_____

_____

_____

_____

_____

_____

_____

_____

_____

_____

_____

_____

_____

Father God, I thank You for
holding these things together:

_____

_____

_____

_____

_____

_____

_____

I love You for_____

_____

_____

_____

_____

_____

_____

_____

Sometimes I want to rage
against You when I am dealing
with_____

_____

_____

_____

_____

_____

_____

_____

_____

_____

Forgive me for_____

_____

_____

_____

_____

_____

_____

_____

_____

_____

_____

_____

"For He will give His angels charge concerning you, To guard you in all your ways."
PSALMS 91:11 (NASB)

JAN'S THOT

Are you aware that angels are with you today? They have charge of you and are diligently watching over you. That should be a source of comfort on your journey!

My personal thoughts are...

_____

_____

_____

_____

_____

_____

_____

_____

_____

_____

_____

_____

Heavenly Father, thank You for putting angels in charge of me.

Knowing that angels are guarding me is a comfort when...

_____
_____
_____
_____
_____
_____
_____
_____
_____

I pray for my precious loved ones:

_____
_____
_____
_____
_____
_____
_____
_____
_____
_____

I ask You to...

_____
_____
_____
_____
_____

I want to understand about...

_____
_____
_____
_____
_____
_____

I love You for_____

_____
_____
_____
_____
_____
_____

"If you need wisdom—if you want to know what God wants you to do—ask him, and he will gladly tell you. He will not resent your asking. But when you ask him, be sure that you really expect him to answer, for a doubtful mind is as unsettled as a wave of the sea that is driven and tossed by the wind."

JAMES 1:5, 6 (NLT)

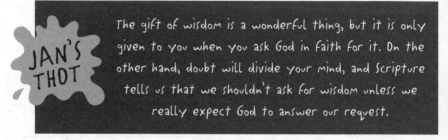

JAN'S THOT

The gift of wisdom is a wonderful thing, but it is only given to you when you ask God in faith for it. On the other hand, doubt will divide your mind, and Scripture tells us that we shouldn't ask for wisdom unless we really expect God to answer our request.

My personal thoughts are...

_____

_____

_____

_____

_____

_____

_____

_____

_____

_____

_____

_____

Father, I want to believe with full faith that You are answering my prayer regarding_____

_____

_____

_____

_____

_____

_____

I need wisdom for _____

_____

_____

_____

_____

_____

_____

I long for You to move in...

_____

_____

_____

_____

_____

_____

I pray for_____

_____

_____

_____

_____

_____

_____

_____

_____

_____

I love You for_____

_____

_____

_____

_____

_____

_____

_____

_____

_____

_____

_____

_____

_____

"For we must all appear before the judgment seat of Christ, that each one may be recompensed for his deeds in the body, according to what he has done, whether good or bad."

2 CORINTHIANS 5:10 (NASB)

JAN'S THOT

Standing before the judgment seat of Christ is a solo event. You can't look to the left or the right and say, "but what about her?" It is a required appearance, a solitary appointment, and it will reveal the truth. Do you ever think about the judgment seat of Christ?

What are your thoughts on the judgment seat of Christ?

_____

_____

_____

_____

_____

_____

_____

_____

_____

_____

_____

_____

Lord God, I long to be able to stand before You
on my own two feet.

Please show me where I am
depending on others to make
me look good to You.

_____
_____
_____
_____
_____
_____
_____
_____

I love You for_____
_____
_____
_____
_____
_____
_____
_____
_____
_____

Please show me
where I am blaming
others.

_____
_____
_____
_____
_____
_____
_____
_____

Forgive me for...

_____
_____
_____
_____
_____
_____
_____

"The LORD is good to those who wait for Him, To the person who seeks Him."

LAMENTATIONS 3:25 (NASB)

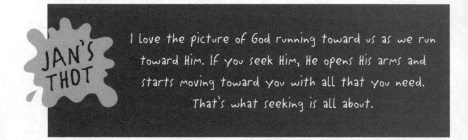

JAN'S THOT

I love the picture of God running toward us as we run toward Him. If you seek Him, He opens His arms and starts moving toward you with all that you need. That's what seeking is all about.

My personal thoughts are...

_____

_____

_____

_____

_____

_____

_____

_____

_____

_____

_____

_____

_____

_____

Father God, I want to seek You with my whole heart. To me that means...

_____
_____
_____
_____

I look to You to come running with...

_____
_____
_____
_____
_____

My greatest heart burden is...

_____
_____
_____
_____
_____
_____

I love You for _____
_____
_____
_____
_____
_____

I lift these people before you...

1 _____
2 _____
3 _____
4 _____
5 _____
6 _____
7 _____
8 _____
9 _____
10 _____
11 _____
12 _____
13 _____
14 _____
15 _____

"Who is the man who fears the LORD? He will instruct him in the way he should choose. His soul will abide in prosperity, And his descendants will inherit the land. The secret of the LORD is for those who fear Him, And He will make them know His covenant."

PSALMS 25:12–14 (NASB)

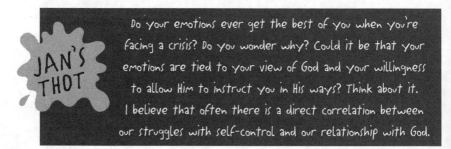

JAN'S THOT

Do your emotions ever get the best of you when you're facing a crisis? Do you wonder why? Could it be that your emotions are tied to your view of God and your willingness to allow Him to instruct you in His ways? Think about it. I believe that often there is a direct correlation between our struggles with self-control and our relationship with God.

My personal thoughts are...

_____

_____

_____

_____

_____

_____

_____

_____

_____

_____

_____

_____

_____

Father God, I want my emotions to be healthy and prosperous.

Instruct me in the way I
should go in regard to

_____

_____

_____

_____

_____

_____

_____

_____

I want to know how to fear
You in the right way. Would
You please show what healthy
fear looks like?

_____

_____

_____

_____

_____

_____

_____

I pray for_____

_____

_____

_____

_____

_____

_____

_____

_____

_____

I love You for_____

_____

_____

_____

_____

_____

_____

_____

_____

_____

Today's Date _____

"And let us not lose heart in doing good,
for in due time we shall reap if we do not grow weary."
GALATIANS 6:9 (NASB)

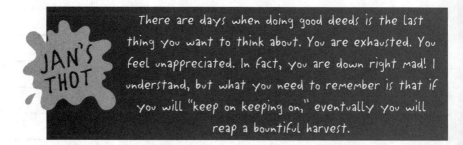

JAN'S THOT

There are days when doing good deeds is the last thing you want to think about. You are exhausted. You feel unappreciated. In fact, you are down right mad! I understand, but what you need to remember is that if you will "keep on keeping on," eventually you will reap a bountiful harvest.

What things have frustrated you recently?

_____

_____

_____

_____

_____

_____

_____

_____

_____

_____

_____

_____

Father God, I am tired of doing good in
this situation:

_____
_____
_____
_____
_____
_____
_____

I ask You to give
me the strength I
need to continue to
love...

1 _____
2 _____
3 _____
4 _____
5 _____
6 _____

Please, work in me in regard to...

7 _____
8 _____

_____
_____
_____
_____
_____
_____

9 _____
10 _____
11 _____
12 _____
13 _____
14 _____
15 _____

I love You for_____
_____
_____
_____
_____
_____
_____

"For I am confident of this very thing, that He who began a good work in you will perfect it until the day of Christ Jesus."

PHILIPPIANS 1:6 (NASB)

JAN'S THOT

If God has started the good work of salvation in you, He will complete it! That is a wonderful reminder for those days when you wonder if God even exists!

My personal thoughts are...

_____

_____

_____

_____

_____

_____

_____

_____

_____

_____

_____

_____

_____

Father God, there are days I feel You are far away or don't even exist. I ask You to make Yourself real to me. I pray for my family: _____

_____

_____

_____

_____

_____

_____

_____

_____

I pray that You will make Yourself real to my family and friends in ways they can hold on to. I love You for being patient and for:

_____

_____

_____

_____

_____

_____

_____

_____

I pray for my friends:

1 _____

2 _____

3 _____

4 _____

5 _____

6 _____

7 _____

8 _____

9 _____

10 _____

11 _____

12 _____

13 _____

14 _____

15 _____

"Therefore, if your enemy hungers, feed him; if he thirsts, give him a drink; for in so doing you will heap coals of fire on his head. Do not be overcome with evil but overcome evil with good."

ROMANS 12:20, 21 (NKJV)

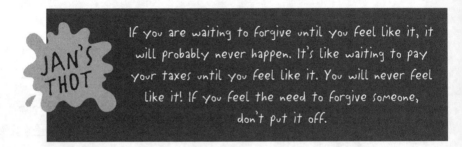

JAN'S THOT

If you are waiting to forgive until you feel like it, it will probably never happen. It's like waiting to pay your taxes until you feel like it. You will never feel like it! If you feel the need to forgive someone, don't put it off.

Have you ever had good intentions of forgiving someone, yet failed to get around to it?...

_____

_____

_____

_____

_____

_____

_____

_____

_____

_____

_____

_____

Father God, thank You for forgiving me.

_____
~~~~~~~~~~~~~~~~~~~~~~~~~~~
~~~~~~~~~~~~~~~~~~~~~~~~~~~
~~~~~~~~~~~~~~~~~~~~~~~~~~~
~~~~~~~~~~~~~~~~~~~~~~~~~~~
~~~~~~~~~~~~~~~~~~~~~~~~~~~
~~~~~~~~~~~~~~~~~~~~~~~~~~~
~~~~~~~~~~~~~~~~~~~~~~~~~~~
~~~~~~~~~~~~~~~~~~~~~~~~~~~
~~~~~~~~~~~~~~~~~~~~~~~~~~~

I want to forgive

_____

and demonstrate Your character through _____

~~~~~~~~~~~~~~~~~~~~~~~~~~~
~~~~~~~~~~~~~~~~~~~~~~~~~~~
~~~~~~~~~~~~~~~~~~~~~~~~~~~
~~~~~~~~~~~~~~~~~~~~~~~~~~~
~~~~~~~~~~~~~~~~~~~~~~~~~~~
~~~~~~~~~~~~~~~~~~~~~~~~~~~

I want to overcome the situation with good. Give me the idea of what to do.

~~~~~~~~~~~~~~~~~~~~~~~~~~~
~~~~~~~~~~~~~~~~~~~~~~~~~~~
~~~~~~~~~~~~~~~~~~~~~~~~~~~
~~~~~~~~~~~~~~~~~~~~~~~~~~~
~~~~~~~~~~~~~~~~~~~~~~~~~~~
~~~~~~~~~~~~~~~~~~~~~~~~~~~
~~~~~~~~~~~~~~~~~~~~~~~~~~~
~~~~~~~~~~~~~~~~~~~~~~~~~~~

I love You for_____

~~~~~~~~~~~~~~~~~~~~~~~~~~~
~~~~~~~~~~~~~~~~~~~~~~~~~~~
~~~~~~~~~~~~~~~~~~~~~~~~~~~
~~~~~~~~~~~~~~~~~~~~~~~~~~~
~~~~~~~~~~~~~~~~~~~~~~~~~~~
~~~~~~~~~~~~~~~~~~~~~~~~~~~
~~~~~~~~~~~~~~~~~~~~~~~~~~~

"The LORD has done great things for us; We are glad."

PSALM 126:3 (NASB)

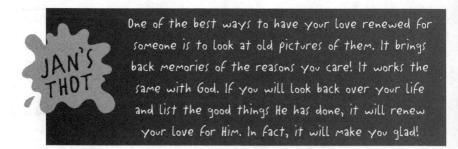

JAN'S THOT

One of the best ways to have your love renewed for someone is to look at old pictures of them. It brings back memories of the reasons you care! It works the same with God. If you will look back over your life and list the good things He has done, it will renew your love for Him. In fact, it will make you glad!

My personal thoughts are...

_____

_____

_____

_____

_____

_____

_____

_____

_____

_____

_____

_____

_____

_____

Lord God, I remember these
things with gratitude:

_____
_____
_____
_____
_____
_____
_____
_____
_____
_____
_____

I thank You for what I believe
You are doing now in regard
to: _____

_____
_____
_____
_____
_____
_____
_____
_____
_____
_____
_____

I am glad because _____

_____
_____
_____
_____
_____
_____
_____
_____
_____
_____
_____

I love You for _____

_____
_____
_____
_____
_____
_____
_____
_____
_____
_____
_____
_____

Today's Date _____

"Unless the LORD builds the house, They labor in vain who build it; Unless the LORD guards the city, The watchman keeps awake in vain. It is vain for you to rise up early, To retire late, To eat the bread of painful labors; For He gives to His beloved even in his sleep."

PSALM 127:1, 2 (NASB)

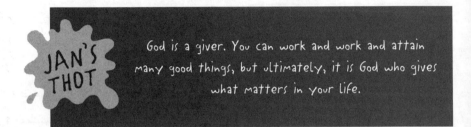

JAN'S THOT

God is a giver. You can work and work and attain many good things, but ultimately, it is God who gives what matters in your life.

My personal thoughts are...

_____
_____
_____
_____
_____
_____
_____
_____
_____
_____
_____
_____
_____

Lord God, thank You for giving me...

_____

_____

_____

_____

_____

_____

I ask for _____

_____

_____

_____

_____

_____

_____

I love You for _____

_____

_____

_____

_____

_____

_____

_____

I pray for these precious loved ones:

1 _____

2 _____

3 _____

4 _____

5 _____

6 _____

7 _____

8 _____

9 _____

10 _____

11 _____

12 _____

13 _____

14 _____

15 _____

"Consider it all joy, my brethren, when you encounter various trials, knowing that the testing of your faith produces endurance. And let endurance have its perfect result, that you may be perfect and complete, lacking in nothing."

JAMES 1:2–4 (NASB)

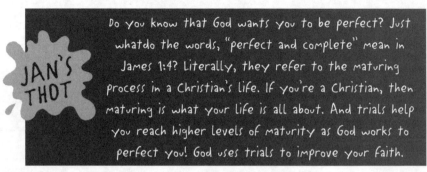

JAN'S THOT

Do you know that God wants you to be perfect? Just what do the words, "perfect and complete" mean in James 1:4? Literally, they refer to the maturing process in a Christian's life. If you're a Christian, then maturing is what your life is all about. And trials help you reach higher levels of maturity as God works to perfect you! God uses trials to improve your faith.

My personal thoughts are...

_____

_____

_____

_____

_____

_____

_____

_____

_____

_____

_____

_____

Father God, I come to You with my prayer today.

I want to grow in these areas:

_____
_____
_____
_____
_____
_____
_____
_____
_____
_____

I love You for _____

_____
_____
_____
_____
_____
_____
_____
_____
_____
_____

Show me how to go through...

_____
_____
_____
_____
_____
_____
_____
_____

I ask You to...

_____
_____
_____
_____
_____
_____
_____
_____

"'And You shall love the Lord your God with all your heart, and with all your soul, and with all your mind, and with all your strength.' The second is this, 'You shall love your neighbor as yourself.' There is no other commandment greater than these."

MARK 12:30, 31 (NASB)

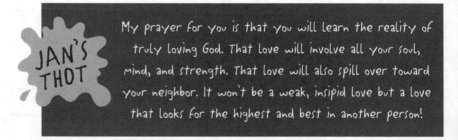

JAN'S THOT

My prayer for you is that you will learn the reality of truly loving God. That love will involve all your soul, mind, and strength. That love will also spill over toward your neighbor. It won't be a weak, insipid love but a love that looks for the highest and best in another person!

How is your love for God right now? How about your neighbor?

_____

_____

_____

_____

_____

_____

_____

_____

_____

_____

_____

Father, show me how to love my neighbor.

_____

_____

_____

_____

_____

_____

I find these things difficult:

_____

_____

_____

_____

_____

_____

I pray this for my neighbor:

_____

_____

_____

_____

_____

_____

_____

_____

I lift these neighbors before you...

1 _____

2 _____

3 _____

4 _____

5 _____

6 _____

7 _____

8 _____

9 _____

10 _____

11 _____

12 _____

13 _____

14 _____

15 _____

*"Do not misuse the name of the LORD your God. The LORD will not let you go
unpunished if you misuse his name."*

EXODUS 20:7 (NLT)

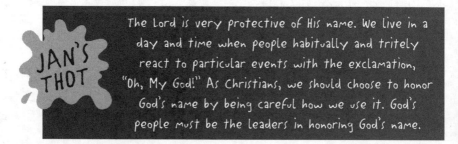

JAN'S THOT

The Lord is very protective of His name. We live in a
day and time when people habitually and tritely
react to particular events with the exclamation,
"Oh, My God!" As Christians, we should choose to honor
God's name by being careful how we use it. God's
people must be the leaders in honoring God's name.

Write down your feelings about God's name.

_____

_____

_____

_____

_____

_____

_____

_____

_____

_____

_____

_____

Oh, Lord God, I pray for You to put a holy
reverence in my life. Remind me to...

_____
_____
_____
_____
_____
_____
_____
_____
_____
_____
_____

I love You for _____
_____
_____
_____
_____
_____
_____
_____
_____
_____
_____
_____

I pray that these
people would learn
to revere You:

1 _____
2 _____
3 _____
4 _____
5 _____
6 _____
7 _____
8 _____
9 _____
10 _____
11 _____
12 _____
13 _____
14 _____
15 _____

"Then a poor widow came by and dropped in two pennies. 'I assure you,' he said, 'this poor widow has given more than all the rest of them. For they have given a tiny part of their surplus, but she, poor as she is, has given everything she has.'"

LUKE 21:2–4 (NLT)

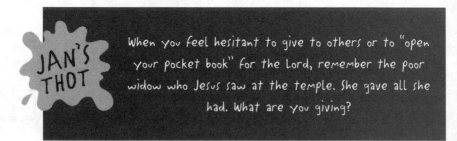

JAN'S THOT

When you feel hesitant to give to others or to "open your pocket book" for the Lord, remember the poor widow who Jesus saw at the temple. She gave all she had. What are you giving?

My personal thoughts on giving are...

_____
_____
_____
_____
_____
_____
_____
_____
_____
_____
_____
_____

Lord God, show me what I can give.

_____
_____
_____
_____
_____
_____
_____
_____
_____

I have given _____
to:
_____
_____
_____
_____
_____
_____
_____
_____
_____
_____
_____

I have seen Your hand in...

_____
_____
_____
_____
_____
_____
_____
_____
_____
_____

I love You for_____
_____
_____
_____
_____
_____
_____
_____
_____
_____
_____

"The steps of a good man are ordered by the Lord, and He delights in his way. Though he fall, he shall not be utterly cast down; for the Lord upholds him with His Hand."

PSALM 37:23, 24 (NKJV)

JAN'S THOT

Even as a Christian, you are prone to stumble and fall; however, the Lord has promised to pick you up. Why not jot down a few notes about when the Lord upheld you? Remember, the goodness of God is a good thing to record.

My personal thoughts are...

_____

_____

_____

_____

_____

_____

_____

_____

_____

_____

_____

_____

Holy Father, I want to honor you.

Please show me what I can do.

I seek Your wisdom for...

_____
_____
_____
_____
_____
_____
_____
_____
_____

_____
_____
_____
_____
_____
_____
_____
_____
_____

I pray for _____

I praise you for your goodness:

_____
_____
_____
_____
_____
_____
_____
_____
_____

_____
_____
_____
_____
_____
_____
_____
_____
_____

"Anyone who listens to the word but does not do what it says is like a man who looks at his face in a mirror and, after looking at himself, goes away and immediately forgets what he looks like. But the man who looks intently into the perfect law that gives freedom, and continues to do this, . . . he will be blessed in what he does."

JAMES 1:22–25 (NIV)

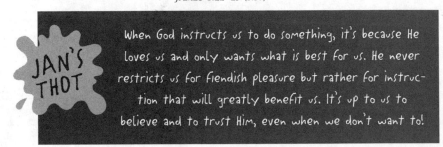

JAN'S THOT

When God instructs us to do something, it's because He loves us and only wants what is best for us. He never restricts us for fiendish pleasure but rather for instruction that will greatly benefit us. It's up to us to believe and to trust Him, even when we don't want to!

My personal thoughts are...

_____

_____

_____

_____

_____

_____

_____

_____

_____

_____

_____

_____

_____

_____

Father, I am struggling with...

I ask for the grace to obey.

_____
_____
_____
_____
_____
_____
_____
_____
_____
_____
_____

I want to
_____,
but You have said_____
_____
_____
_____
_____
_____
_____
_____
_____
_____
_____

I love You for _____
_____
_____
_____
_____
_____
_____
_____
_____
_____
_____

"He was with God in the beginning. Through him all things were made; without him nothing was made that has been made. In him was life, and that life was the light of men."

JOHN 1:2–4 (NIV)

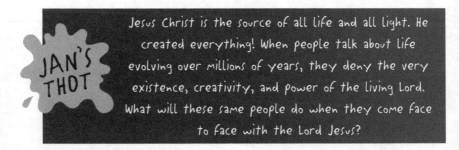

JAN'S THOT

Jesus Christ is the source of all life and all light. He created everything! When people talk about life evolving over millions of years, they deny the very existence, creativity, and power of the living Lord. What will these same people do when they come face to face with the Lord Jesus?

On a more personal level, what are you doing with the Lord Jesus today?

_____

_____

_____

_____

_____

_____

_____

_____

_____

_____

_____

Father God, I thank You for the gift of Jesus.

_____
_____
_____
_____
_____
_____
_____
_____
_____
_____
_____
_____

I love You for...

_____
_____
_____
_____
_____
_____
_____
_____
_____

I pray that You will make the gift of Jesus more and more real to...

1 _____
2 _____
3 _____
4 _____
5 _____
6 _____
7 _____
8 _____
9 _____
10 _____
11 _____
12 _____
13 _____
14 _____
15 _____
16 _____
17 _____
18 _____
19 _____
20 _____
21 _____

"I will bless the LORD who has counseled me; Indeed, my mind instructs me in the night."

PSALM 16:7 (NASB)

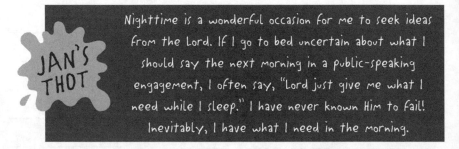

JAN'S THOT

Nighttime is a wonderful occasion for me to seek ideas from the Lord. If I go to bed uncertain about what I should say the next morning in a public-speaking engagement, I often say, "Lord just give me what I need while I sleep." I have never known Him to fail! Inevitably, I have what I need in the morning.

Try seeking ideas from the Lord tonight as you go to bed. Tomorrow morning, come back to this page and jot down what ideas, if any, came to you.

_____

_____

_____

_____

_____

_____

_____

_____

_____

_____

_____

Lord God, I need You to counsel me about...

_____

_____

_____

_____

_____

_____

_____

_____

_____

_____

I thank You for Your counsel
to me about...

_____

_____

_____

_____

_____

_____

_____

_____

_____

When I go to sleep tonight,
would You...

_____

_____

_____

_____

_____

_____

_____

_____

_____

_____?

I love you for...

_____

_____

_____

_____

_____

_____

_____

_____

_____

_____

"For whatever God says to us is full of living power: it is sharper than the sharpest dagger, cutting swift and deep into our innermost thoughts and desires with all their parts, exposing us for what we really are."

HEBREWS 4:12 (TLB)

JAN'S THOT

Whenever God speaks to us through His Word, He touches the deepest part of our lives. Amazingly, His Word has the ability to go to a part of our being where nothing else can go. That's why it is so important to read the Bible with much anticipation!

My personal thoughts are...

_____

_____

_____

_____

_____

_____

_____

_____

_____

_____

_____

_____

_____

Lord God, thank You for Your Word and teaching me.

I praise you for...

_____

_____

_____

_____

_____

_____

_____

_____

_____

I want to understand...

_____

_____

_____

_____

_____

_____

_____

_____

_____

_____

I pray that _____

_____

_____

_____

would know You.

I love you for_____

_____

_____

_____

_____

_____

_____

_____

_____

_____

_____

_____

"Whoever guarantees to pay somebody else's loan will suffer. It is safer to avoid such promises."
PROVERBS 11:15 (NCV)

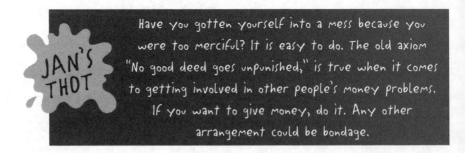

JAN'S THOT

Have you gotten yourself into a mess because you were too merciful? It is easy to do. The old axiom "No good deed goes unpunished," is true when it comes to getting involved in other people's money problems. If you want to give money, do it. Any other arrangement could be bondage.

My personal thoughts are...

_____
_____
_____
_____
_____
_____
_____
_____
_____
_____
_____
_____

father God, show me where and to whom
You want me to give.

_____
_____
_____
_____
_____
_____
_____
_____

I pray for_____
financial need.

I praise you for _____
_____
_____
_____
_____
_____

I love You for _____
_____
_____
_____
_____

I ask You to bless...

1 _____
2 _____
3 _____
4 _____
5 _____
6 _____
7 _____
8 _____
9 _____
10 _____
11 _____
12 _____
13 _____
14 _____
15 _____

"O my people, may you live good and perfect lives before the Lord our God; may you always obey his laws and commandments, just as you are doing today."

1 KINGS 8:61 (TLB)

JAN'S THOT

Having a heart for God means you choose His way over everyone else's. He loves it when we have a heart for Him. He will spare none of His blessings when we focus only on Him and choose His way.

My personal thoughts are...

_____

_____

_____

_____

_____

_____

_____

_____

_____

_____

_____

_____

_____

Father God, I want to live a "good and perfect" life before You.

However, I feel limited in these areas:

_____

_____

_____

_____

_____

_____

_____

Will You show me how to over-come my tendencies to go against You?

_____

_____

_____

_____

_____

_____

_____

_____

I pray for_____

_____

_____

_____

_____

_____

_____

_____

_____

I love You for_____

_____

_____

_____

_____

_____

_____

_____

_____

"Oh, how grateful and thankful I am to the Lord because he is so good. I will sing praise to the name of the Lord who is above all lords."

PSALM 7:17 (TLB)

JAN'S THOT

Can you name three things that you immediately think of when you think of the goodness of God? Why not write a little song about the goodness of God to hum around the house? I believe it would bring Him pleasure.

1.) _____
_____
_____
_____

2.) _____
_____
_____
_____

3.) _____
_____
_____
_____

Lord God, You are so good.

I love You for...

_____
_____
_____
_____
_____
_____
_____
_____

I ask You to work in...

_____
_____
_____
_____
_____
_____
_____
_____
_____

I pray that I will _____

_____
_____
_____
_____
_____
_____
_____
_____
_____
_____
_____
_____
_____
_____

Would You bless_____

_____
_____?

"The words of a good person give life, like a fountain of water, but the words of the wicked contain nothing but violence."

PROVERBS 10:11 (NCV)

JAN'S THOT

Everyone needs to be reminded that good words are like refreshing water in a desert. You probably have a friend who needs your encouraging words to water her soul today. Today would be a good day to cheer and support that person. At the end of the day, jot down how beneficial that time of encouraging was to you and your friend.

My personal thoughts are...

_____

_____

_____

_____

_____

_____

_____

_____

_____

_____

_____

_____

Lord God, You have spoken these healing
words to me:

_____

_____

_____

_____

_____

I pray for_____

_____

_____

_____

_____

I ask You to_____

_____

_____

_____

_____

_____

_____

I love You for_____

_____

_____

_____

Give me healing
words to speak to...

1 _____

2 _____

3 _____

4 _____

5 _____

6 _____

7 _____

8 _____

9 _____

10 _____

11 _____

12 _____

13 _____

14 _____

15 _____

"Doing right brings freedom to honest people, but those who are not trustworthy will be caught by their own desires.

PROVERBS 11:6 (NCV)

JAN'S THOT

If you have a choice between doing what is right and doing what is not necessarily right, but seemingly expedient, choose the right thing. I used to ask audiences, "When is it right to do right?" I was always amazed how Christian audiences could be the slowest to answer that question, like it was a trick. Right is right and there is great freedom in choosing it!

My personal thoughts are...

_____

_____

_____

_____

_____

_____

_____

_____

_____

_____

_____

_____

Father, I thank You for giving me the
Holy Spirit who teaches me what is
right. Would You make me sensitive to
what He is saying to me about...

_____

_____

_____

_____

_____

_____

_____?

I pray that _____

will _____

_____

_____

_____

_____

I love You for
_____

_____

_____

_____

_____

_____

_____

_____

Bless these people
for their kindness:

1 _____

2 _____

3 _____

4 _____

5 _____

6 _____

7 _____

8 _____

9 _____

10 _____

11 _____

12 _____

13 _____

14 _____

15 _____

"As the deer pants for the water brooks, So pants my soul for You, O God. My soul thirsts for God, for the living God. When shall I come and appear before God?"
PSALMS 42:1, 2 (NKJV)

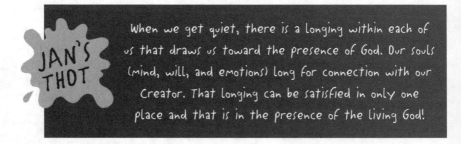

JAN'S THOT

When we get quiet, there is a longing within each of us that draws us toward the presence of God. Our souls (mind, will, and emotions) long for connection with our Creator. That longing can be satisfied in only one place and that is in the presence of the living God!

My personal thoughts are...

_____

_____

_____

_____

_____

_____

_____

_____

_____

_____

_____

_____

Father, I long for You to speak
to me about_____

_____

_____

_____

_____

_____

_____

_____

_____

_____

I love You for_____

_____

_____

_____

_____

_____

_____

_____

_____

_____

_____

_____

I want to say this to You:

_____

_____

_____

_____

_____

_____

_____

_____

_____

_____

_____

I praise you for...

_____

_____

_____

_____

_____

_____

_____

_____

_____

_____

"Through You we will push down our enemies; Through Your name we will trample those who rise up against us. For I will not trust in my bow, Nor shall my sword save me."

PSALM 44:5, 6 (NKJV)

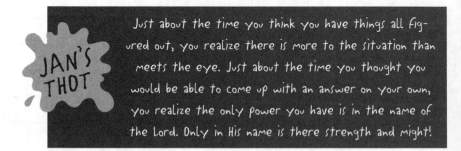

JAN'S THOT

Just about the time you think you have things all figured out, you realize there is more to the situation than meets the eye. Just about the time you thought you would be able to come up with an answer on your own, you realize the only power you have is in the name of the Lord. Only in His name is there strength and might!

My personal thoughts are...

_____
_____
_____
_____
_____
_____
_____
_____
_____
_____
_____
_____
_____

Father, I come to You in the name of Jesus.

I ask You to conquer...

_____
_____
_____
_____
_____
_____
_____
_____
_____
_____
_____

I ask for help with...

_____
_____
_____
_____
_____
_____
_____
_____
_____
_____

I love You for_____

_____
_____
_____
_____
_____
_____
_____
_____

Other matters I want to discuss with You:

_____
_____
_____
_____
_____
_____
_____
_____
_____
_____

"Fools quickly show that they are upset, but the wise ignore insults."
PROVERBS 12:16 (NCV)

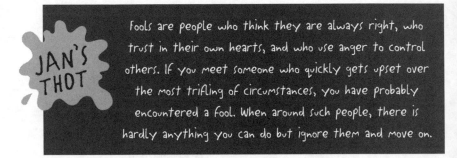

JAN'S THOT

Fools are people who think they are always right, who trust in their own hearts, and who use anger to control others. If you meet someone who quickly gets upset over the most trifling of circumstances, you have probably encountered a fool. When around such people, there is hardly anything you can do but ignore them and move on.

My personal thoughts are...

_____

_____

_____

_____

_____

_____

_____

_____

_____

_____

_____

_____

Lord, show me what my angry outbursts tell about me.

I know I hate it when...

_____
_____
_____
_____
_____
_____
_____
_____
_____
_____

I ask You to show me how to
ignore_____

_____
_____
_____
_____
_____
_____
_____
_____
_____

I pray for_____

_____
_____
_____
_____
_____
_____
_____
_____
_____
_____
_____

I love You for_____

_____
_____
_____
_____
_____
_____
_____
_____
_____
_____

"Listen, O daughter, Consider and incline your ear; Forget your own people also, and your father's house; So the King will greatly desire your beauty; Because He is your Lord, worship Him."

PSALMS 45:10, 11 (NKJV)

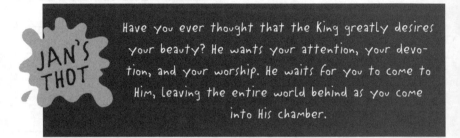

JAN'S THOT

Have you ever thought that the King greatly desires your beauty? He wants your attention, your devotion, and your worship. He waits for you to come to Him, leaving the entire world behind as you come into His chamber.

My personal thoughts are...

_____

_____

_____

_____

_____

_____

_____

_____

_____

_____

_____

_____

_____

My King, I long to know how to worship You.

I love You and I desire Your
beauty.

~~~~~~
~~~~~~
~~~~~~
~~~~~~
~~~~~~
~~~~~~
~~~~~~
~~~~~~
~~~~~~
~~~~~~
~~~~~~
~~~~~~

Teach me to love You.

~~~~~~
~~~~~~
~~~~~~
~~~~~~
~~~~~~
~~~~~~
~~~~~~
~~~~~~
~~~~~~
~~~~~~
~~~~~~
~~~~~~

"But I am like an olive tree flourishing in the house of God; I trust in God's unfailing love for ever and ever. I will praise you forever for what you have done; in your name I will hope, for your name is good. I will praise you in the presence of your saints."

PSALMS 52:8, 9 (NIV)

JAN'S THOT

The decision to praise the Lord, no matter what, is a bold statement of trust in God that always brings a smile to His lips! When we praise, we feel His pleasure.

My personal thoughts are...

_____

_____

_____

_____

_____

_____

_____

_____

_____

_____

_____

_____

_____

Lord, I trust You for _____

_____

_____

_____

_____

_____

_____

_____

_____

I lift these people before you...

1 _____

2 _____

3 _____

4 _____

5 _____

6 _____

7 _____

I love You for _____

_____

_____

_____

_____

_____

_____

8 _____

9 _____

10 _____

11 _____

12 _____

13 _____

14 _____

15 _____

I want to tell everyone that...

_____

_____

_____

_____

_____

_____

_____

_____

Today's Date _____

"When a wicked man dies, his hope perishes; all he expected from his power comes to nothing."
PROVERBS 11:7 (NIV)

JAN'S THOT

Isn't it amazing how priorities change when someone dies? Have you thought what will happen when you die? What will the people you love remember most about you? Make these questions a point of reflection this week.

My personal thoughts are...

_____
_____
_____
_____
_____
_____
_____
_____
_____
_____
_____
_____
_____
_____

Father God, I believe these
things are important to You
and to me:

_____

_____

_____

_____

_____

_____

_____

I love You for _____

_____

_____

_____

_____

_____

_____

_____

_____

_____

_____

_____

_____

_____

_____

I pray for_____

_____

_____

_____

_____

_____

_____

_____

_____

I praise You for_____

_____

_____

_____

_____

_____

_____

_____

_____

_____

_____

_____

_____

_____

_____

"One man gives freely, yet gains even more; another withholds unduly, but comes to poverty. A generous man will prosper; he who refreshes others will himself be refreshed."
PROVERBS 11:24, 25 (NIV)

JAN'S THOT

There is a wonderful law of giving that ripples through Scripture. When you give, you always gain. You may not get back exactly what you have given but you will be blessed in ways you couldn't imagine.

My personal thoughts are...

_____

_____

_____

_____

_____

_____

_____

_____

_____

_____

_____

_____

_____

Lord God, You have given me so much. I thank You for:

_____
_____
_____
_____
_____
_____
_____
_____
_____
_____
_____
_____

I love You for_____
_____
_____
_____
_____
_____
_____
_____
_____
_____
_____
_____

I pray for wisdom in what to give to...

1 _____
2 _____
3 _____
4 _____
5 _____
6 _____
7 _____
8 _____
9 _____
10 _____
11 _____
12 _____
13 _____
14 _____
15 _____

Today's Date _____

"Be sure you know the condition of your flocks, give careful attention to your herds;
for riches do not endure forever, and a crown is not secure for all generations."
PROVERBS 27:23, 24 (NIV)

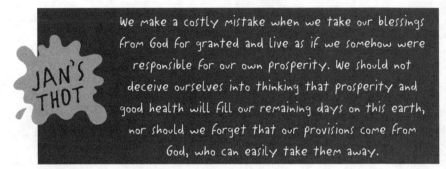

JAN'S THOT

We make a costly mistake when we take our blessings from God for granted and live as if we somehow were responsible for our own prosperity. We should not deceive ourselves into thinking that prosperity and good health will fill our remaining days on this earth, nor should we forget that our provisions come from God, who can easily take them away.

My personal thoughts are...

_____

_____

_____

_____

_____

_____

_____

_____

_____

_____

_____

_____

Lord God, help me to remember how far I've come.

I remember_____
_____
_____
_____
_____
_____
_____
_____
_____
_____
_____

I love You for_____
_____
_____
_____
_____
_____
_____
_____
_____
_____
_____
_____

These people have been instrumental in my spiritual growth...

1 _____
2 _____
3 _____
4 _____
5 _____
6 _____
7 _____
8 _____
9 _____
10 _____
11 _____
12 _____
13 _____
14 _____